SHARK-INFESTED WATERS

Michael Whitehall

TIMEWELL
PRESS

First published in the UK in 2007 by Timewell Press
Copyright © Michael Whitehall 2007

The right of Michael Whitehall to be identified as the author
of this work has been asserted by him in accordance with
the Copyright, Designs and Patents Act, 1988.

A catalogue record for this title is available from
the British Library.

ISBN-13: 978-1-85725-215-6

Typeset by TW Typesetting, Plymouth, Devon

Printed and bound in Great Britain by
William Clowes Ltd, Beccles, Suffolk

Timewell Press Limited
10 Porchester Terrace
London W2 3TL
United Kingdom

Every effort has been made to trace copyright holders and we apologize
in advance for any unintentional omission. We would be pleased to
insert the appropriate acknowledgement in any subsequent edition.

Contents

For Hilary, Jack, Molly and Barney

Acknowledgements

Without Hugh Massingberd's encouragement, I would never have written this book; and without his timely introduction to Andreas Campomar and Gerard Noel, it would never have been published. Andreas seamlessly combined the roles of publisher, editor and literary adviser with great aplomb.

As a first-time writer, I have needed constant help and advice; this I have received in abundance from Gyles and Michèle Brandreth, Christopher Matthew, Nigel Williams, Edwin and Anne Mullins, Jennifer Laidlaw, Conrad Williams and Jane Mays. My thanks to them all, and to Neil Stacy who read the manuscript and gave me much valuable guidance. I must also salute my son Jack for his brilliant, original and skilful illustrations.

Sadly, I have no agent to grovel to, so I reserve my special thanks for Hilary who has put up with me for over twenty years, and miraculously continues to do so. She even laughs at my anecdotal ramblings, which she has heard a thousand times before. To describe her as 'long-suffering' would be wholly inadequate. I dedicate this book to her and our wonderful children.

'Actors live in fear of being resented by their agents for taking 90 per cent of the money they earn'

I was on holiday in Spain with Judi Dench and her husband, Michael Williams.

During supper in Puerto Banus, Judi slipped away from the table and returned with a present for me.

A set of shark's teeth.

'*Dentadura de Tiburón*,' said Judi. 'Very appropriate for an agent. Put them on your desk.'

They've been there ever since.

Prologue

The trouble with St John's Church, Withyham, was that it wasn't in Withyham. There was a church in Withyham but it wasn't St John's, which was in the middle of the Ashdown Forest, tucked away in the undergrowth. There were a lot of late arrivals at our wedding. The best man, Nigel Havers, arrived just as the service began, so there was no help from him in keeping the bridegroom calm and relaxed. The bride, Hilary, was late too, but not as late as the best man.

After the service, Nigel told me that he'd had a row with his wife, Caro, about routes, so much so that they had lost their way three times. His newly wedded agent hoped that Nigel would calm down by the time he got to the reception.

There were more late arrivals at the reception held at Hilary's parents' house in Crowborough; as I waited for the presentation queue to form, James Fox beckoned me over to the side of the marquee.

'Have you got a moment?' he asked. 'I just wondered if you'd heard back from Rose about the Spanish film?' (Rose Tobias Shaw was an American casting director with a rather flaky reputation.)

'No I haven't, but I'm sure it will be fine.'

'It's a good part, don't you think? You liked the script, didn't you?'

'Absolutely, James.'

'And it *is* an offer, isn't it?'

'Sure,' I said.

Judi Dench stuck her head around the corner. 'Did you know there's a wedding reception going on in there, Michael?' she said and disappeared.

'Will the money be any good?' asked James.

'Well, I haven't actually talked . . .'

Nigel appeared hot and flustered. 'We got bloody lost again. God, Caro's hopeless at navigating. I said *Crowborough* not Crowhurst. Are you ready to receive?'

'Absolutely,' I replied. 'See you in a moment.'

'Will I get top billing?' said James.

'I'm going to have to dash, James. Can we talk later?'

'Of course we can, Michael. You've got better things to do, I quite understand. But if you hear anything while you're away you will let me know, won't you?'

'Michael, come on,' said Nigel. 'The vicar is boring the pants off Tom Courtenay.'

'It must be a nightmare being an actors' agent,' said John Wells as I walked with him towards the marquee.

2

'Everyone pretending to be your friend when in fact all
they want is for you to get them a decent job with loads
of money.'

'No, no, John,' I replied, 'it's not a nightmare. I love
actors. They're great.'

After the speeches, I was talking to a friend of Hilary's
father.

'It must be very glamorous swanning around the
world, visiting film locations,' he said.

'Yes, there is a bit of that, but most of it's pretty
humdrum and boring; a bit like working in a bank.'

'I'm a bank manager, actually, and I find it very
interesting,' he replied. 'I've just been having a long chat
with Nigel Havers's father's bodyguard, who's thinking
of changing banks. Charming man. Now there's an
interesting job, bodyguard to the Attorney General.'

My mother, Nora, had of course come to the wedding
and spent most of the day looking for Stewart Granger.
She'd never wanted me to be an agent. 'Mucking about
with actors won't get you anywhere, dear,' she used to
say. 'Get yourself a proper job.'

She was bitterly disappointed that I never completed
my articles with Williams & James, Solicitors of Gray's
Inn, failed my Bar exams, and drifted in and out of
various media jobs. It was my lazy streak coming
through, she used to say. In any case, she definitely didn't
like the notion of my being an agent, and it was only

when she heard I was representing Stewart Granger that she began showing some interest in the whole thing. She loved Stewart Granger – though probably not as much as he loved himself – and adored all his films: *The Man in Grey, King Solomon's Mines, Scaramouche, Bhowani Junction.* Now there was a *real* film star.

Unfortunately, Jimmy Granger didn't turn up at the wedding – maybe he got lost – so Nora had to make do with Sandy Gall, another great favourite of hers, but not quite in the same league.

I bumped into Anton Rodgers on my way to the house to change.

'Great wedding, Mike! Remind me where you're going on honeymoon? Sardinia, isn't it?'

'No, the Seychelles, actually, but we're spending a couple of nights in Bath first.'

'Do you mind if I have your numbers . . . y-you know, just in case?'

'Of course, ring me any time.'

'Well I won't disturb you unless it is something urgent. To be honest I need a job. You know it's been three months since I finished the series. I thought this was going to be a really good year but it's turning out to be a disaster.'

As we were changing there was a knock at the door.

'We've got to dash Michael,' said Nigel. 'We're spending the weekend with the parents in Suffolk and at this rate we'll be there at midnight. I'm going to let Caro drive and do my own navigating this time. Give me a call next week . . . you never know, we might have heard back from ITV.'

On our way to the Priory Hotel in Bath, I mused on John Wells's remarks and the fine line between client and friend. Were any of these people really my friends? Or were they just fair-weather friends? With a few exceptions, maybe not friends for life but certainly friends for the life of their next contract.

As Hilary and I lay on the bed talking about the day and getting ready for our first night of wedded bliss, a note was slipped under the door.

Rose Tobias Shaw had called and left a message. They had gone with Lloyd Bridges, but would James be interested in playing the friend? She'd ring me in the morning.

I turned out the light.

1

Keeping Up Appearances

Around the time Adolf Hitler and Hermann Goering were discussing on which British cathedral towns to launch their retaliatory Baedeker raids, Jack and Nora Whitehall were making up their minds where they might rent a house to get away from the London bombs. Unfortunately, Jack and Nora had the same idea as Adolf and Hermann: Exeter.

Jack spent most of the war travelling around the country as a gas instructor in the RAF. When he'd joined up, Nora had pictured him as a dashing pilot with a fur-lined flying jacket and polka-dot silk cravat, though the reality was a desk job based near Taunton with particular responsibility for teaching new recruits to cope with gas attacks. As, of course, there weren't any, Jack could be said to have had a 'bad war'; but at least he was in uniform, unlike his brother Cyril, who was making a fortune selling them to the army.

One of many houses that my parents rented during the

'Nora had pictured Jack as a dashing pilot in a polka-dot silk cravat'

war, and certainly the one from which our family made the swiftest exit, was 60 Rivermead Gardens, Exeter. One night, during an air raid, we were all huddled in the Anderson shelter at the end of the garden when there was an enormous explosion, which knocked the shelter flying. As we staggered out, my mother clutching me to her ample bosom, we saw that 60 Rivermead Gardens had disappeared. We'd had what was appropriately called a 'direct hit'. So much for Nora's notion of a safe haven.

Nora, whose maiden name was Kellond, claimed to be related to the Earl of Egmont, but she was always rather skimpy when it came to the fine detail. The Egmont family name was Perceval; the earldom had been created in Ireland in 1733, and the current earl appeared to live abroad somewhere, though Nora wasn't sure where. As the years went by, the Egmont connection was referred to more frequently; although in her dotage it turned out that it was my father Jack who was apparently related to the Egmonts: an even unlikelier story.

The Kellond girls – Nora had two sisters, Betty and Vera – were brought up in the gentility of Bearsden, a middle-class suburb of Glasgow, in the 1920s. Her mother Elizabeth was a formidable woman with a bosom of Hattie Jacques proportions. But Elizabeth – unlike Hattie – was shy, retiring and a devout Catholic, and her bosom caused her constant embarrassment. Various corset-like garments were strapped across her chest to keep it flat, but, unfortunately, this only caused it to spill out at the sides. Loose-fitting garments were the order of the day for Elizabeth, and she constantly had the look of a woman in the latter stages of pregnancy.

Nora inherited her mother's reserve and also, to an extent, her bosom. Elizabeth's husband, however, was a wholly different proposition. A draper by trade, Arthur overdressed, drank far too much, had a violent temper and spent what little money he had on anything that would show him off to his friends and neighbours. Instead of driving to work, Arthur would ride a white mare, brought to the front door of their suburban villa by a local stable lad. Arthur would then gallop off in his jodhpurs and tweeds to his draper's shop in the centre of Glasgow. It clearly wasn't much fun for the horse – this being the 1920s rather than the 1820s – and there would be much neighing and snorting as he tried to control the animal in the heavy Glasgow traffic. He also owned a convertible Daimler, which he insisted on driving with the hood down in all weathers, and a Sunbeam motorbike with a sidecar. Elizabeth refused to travel in the sidecar, something her daughter, Nora, would do years later when her husband Jack bought his first motorbike; mother and daughter considering it to be the most vulgar form of transport.

Arthur's violent rages, especially when in his cups, proved too much for Elizabeth's delicate disposition. He was often inclined to clear the mantelpiece and the drawing-room table of Elizabeth's collection of bone-china figurines with his riding crop. Elizabeth would then disappear to her room in hysterics, and by the time she reappeared, often twenty-four hours later, her husband had substituted the detritus of the previous night with expensive replacements. Inevitably, the family finances and the marriage ran out of steam. Although Arthur and Elizabeth stayed together for the sake of the children, it was never the most stable of liaisons, the constant flow of crockery across the sitting room causing much upset to the three girls as well as to the neighbours. Lord Egmont certainly wouldn't have approved, nor would he have approved of Arthur's not-so-secret penchant for dressing up in his wife's clothing.

At any social opportunity, Arthur would appear at the dinner table or in the sitting room in full cross-dressing mode: that is apart from the make-up. He didn't actually want to look like a woman, but like a man in woman's clothes. He would often walk down the street in Elizabeth's best hat, coat and shoes, puffing his pipe and fiddling with his moustache. This was Arthur the clown rather than Arthur the transvestite. Either way it caused his wife considerable embarrassment, and being a rather humourless woman, she completely failed to get the joke. It is one thing to call your children embarrassing nicknames in front of their friends, or to trip up in public like Norman Wisdom, but to collect them from school dressed as Norman Bates's mother is no laughing matter.

Needless to say, Arthur's light-hearted transvestism had a profound effect on Nora's development: she suffered acute embarrassment for the rest of her life. In conversation she would never take the lead in anything for fear of getting it wrong. 'I love Rachmaninoff,' she would say, but then try and change the subject in case someone asked her which of his piano concertos she most enjoyed, or whether 'Symphony No. 2' was his defining work. By then, she would be out of her depth.

And perhaps her father's demeanour was ultimately responsible for the fact that she always put the lights out before undressing for bed. Undressing that is into a neck-to-ankle-length nightdress and bed-jacket worn in all weathers. Once when I tentatively enquired as to how she and Jack had babies, having drawn a blank in extracting any information out of the monks of Ampleforth, she told me: 'It happens naturally while your father and I are asleep.' Amazingly, I believed her.

In the late 1950s, when we were on a family holiday in Salcombe, my brother Barry and I went to visit Arthur's cottage outside Kingsbridge. By now, he was in his late seventies – Elizabeth had died some years earlier – and only just able to look after himself. He was expecting us for tea at four o'clock and, as we walked up the garden path, the door flew open. There stood Arthur in a large feathered felt hat, a floral print dress and high heels; he was roaring with laughter and puffing away at his pipe.

★   ★   ★

'At any social opportunity, Arthur would appear in full
cross-dressing mode'

After leaving school, Nora went to the Glasgow School of Art, subsequently getting a job sketching for a fashion catalogue in London. She had a good eye for colour and clearly had talent, but she was never going to make a living as an artist. Soon the paintbrushes were replaced by the typewriter, and then in 1932 she met Jack Whitehall.

The scene of this first meeting was a dinner-dance at a hotel in Croydon. Nora had a flat nearby, which she shared with two other girls – quite a racy arrangement in those innocent days. Jack, on the other hand, was only twenty-two, five years younger than Nora, and lived with his parents in Norbury. It certainly wasn't love at first sight from Nora's point of view. In fact it was Jack's friend Harry Miller to whom Nora first gave her address. But Jack was persistent and, after being turned down on two separate occasions, Nora finally consented to join the Whitehall family. They were married in 1934 in the church in Streatham where, some forty years previously, Jack's parents had wed.

Jack's father, Ernest, was the stuff of Dickensian novels. One of eight children, by the time he was seven he was an orphan. All his siblings had died, his father had been fatally wounded in a pony-and-trap accident and his poor mother – who could blame her – died of grief. A cousin of his father, a rich Birmingham industrialist with a wife and no children, adopted Ernest and ultimately left him his fortune. Charlie Worsley's money ultimately paid for

Barry and me to go to Ampleforth and paid for my first house in Barnes. Even the Whitehall family silver — heavily engraved with a 'W' — was the Worsleys'. Years later I remember visits to Ernest's house in Worthing when he was in his eighties. His wife Edith had died during the war; she had suffered from a floating kidney, which sounded most inconvenient and in her case turned out to be a killer. I remember her only as a very severe-looking woman, always cross, always dressed in black with a penchant for feathers and a very frightening live-looking fox draped around her gangly neck. Ernest was a big bear of a man with thick white hair, and certainly wouldn't have suited his wife's clothes as well as Arthur. He was very deaf, and Barry and I had great fun shouting at each other through his ear trumpet and mouthing sentences to each other across the room, to his increasing annoyance. He also let us play his pianola — a miraculous instrument. At the time I was a great fan of *Sparky*, a book about a boy who had a piano that played itself. I longed for one of these magical instruments, as I was bored to death trying to learn the piano — so rolls of music that could be put into the piano seemed to be a perfect solution.

Ernest's great love, however, was knitting. He would sit in his deep leather armchair with a cigarette in his mouth, the ash growing longer and longer, knitting socks, gloves, jumpers and scarves. I would wait for the ash to fall on to the front of his home-knitted cardigan, which he'd brush off and carry on with the job in hand. He had a live-in housekeeper called Mrs Gale and a chauffeur called Stanley who drove him along the Worthing seafront every day in his elegant, shiny-black Rover 14. Sometimes Barry and I would be allowed to go with him, although I used to get car sick as both he and his chauffeur chain-smoked throughout the journey. On one occasion, having successfully held in my sick until I arrived back at Ernest's house, Stanley braked rather sharply and I delivered a projectile vomit which covered not only the back of Ernest's seat, but also his neck and jacket. He was furious, and I was never invited on one of his seafront drives again. So there were my two grandfathers: one liked dressing up in his wife's clothes and the other liked knitting. I sometimes wonder whether my sons will develop a passion for dressmaking or floral arrangement in later life.

Someone who certainly did not have a feminine side was Uncle Peter. Peter was married to Nora's younger sister Vera, a match which Nora was always rather jealous of. Peter was handsome, had been to a 'good public school' (well, Sutton Valence actually) and was a doctor's son. As an officer in the Royal Artillery, he had had a 'good war': Dunkirk, North Africa, Burma. He had had a very bad time in the jungle and in later life wouldn't allow anything Japanese into the house, which put him at a considerable disadvantage when it came to electrical goods. One Christmas, when he was staying with us, he refused to watch the Queen's Speech because my father had recently acquired a discounted Japanese television set from John Lewis. On leaving the army with the rank of major and getting a job as sales director at a manufacturing company in the Midlands, things went rather downhill, and he ended up as a 'commercial traveller' selling cork tiles. He did however have a company car and an expense account of sorts, so visits to Uncle Peter and Auntie Vera were always looked forward to, even though much time was spent at the local pub, where Peter's hospitality was always at full stretch.

I sometimes wished that Peter and Vera were my parents – their lives always seemed more fun than Jack and Nora's. Although they lived in a 1930s mock-Tudor house in Solihull, there was something racy about Uncle Peter and Auntie Vera. They drank wine with their lunch, in Peter's case rather too much. They seemed to have lots of friends who popped in for morning coffee or lunchtime drinks (nobody ever popped into our house, apart from the man who read the gas meter) and in the afternoon Peter and Vera would sometimes disappear upstairs for an hour or so. Jack and Nora never disappeared upstairs during the day.

After the war, Jack got a job at Marks & Spencer and we lived in a rather grim rented house in Edgware. We didn't, of course, have a car. Jack's brother Cyril had acquired a new Bentley, paid for out of the profits from his military outfitting. Cyril and his formidable wife, Alice, would take Barry and me out for picnics from time to time. I always thought that Uncle Cyril was a bit of a bounder. He even had the look of a bounder: tall, smooth, crinkly hair, always very sleekly dressed, with a penchant for silk shirts and cravats. His voice was smooth too – with a rather louche drawl to it – and whenever I saw him, he would always squeeze a ten-shilling note into my hand. 'Buy something nice for your mother,' he would say; which I'm ashamed to admit I never did.

Cyril seemed to be the complete opposite of his brother Jack and treated him in a rather patronizing way. 'If only you could be successful like Cyril,' Nora would say to Jack which, of course, did wonders for his confidence. 'He and Alice are always flying down to the South of France for long weekends. All I ever get is a Sunday-afternoon run in the car to Westerham for tea,' she moaned.

The arrival of Cyril's Bentley outside our house always caused a bit of a stir and gave Nora's financial credibility a much-needed boost, with Jack hanging on by a thread to his job as assistant manager of Marks & Spencer in Hendon.

As we headed off in the Bentley, the strong smell of the Connolly hide would soon get my stomach churning. By the time we reached the designated stopping point, lunch was the last thing on my mind. This was usually just as well as there were two clear catering options, which Alice strictly adhered to. The chicken, which in those days was still a luxury item, was reserved for themselves and their spoilt and snappy Dachshund, Tina. Barry and I were provided with what I can only describe as *meat* sandwiches. Those were the days when meat, and indeed almost everything else, was cooked to death. Sunday lunch in Edgware was always preceded by the question 'What meat is this?' as Nora put the plate in front of us. The only clue as to whether it was beef, pork or lamb was whether mustard, apple or mint sauce was offered to accompany it. A thick covering of Bisto gravy gave it a bit of flavour but even less of a clue as to what it actually was. The same could be said of the vegetables – always a sad, grisly selection of grey spinach, cabbage and spring greens all merging into one tasteless over-cooked mush.

Towards the end of the war, I was a source of constant embarrassment to Nora by denying the existence of my father. This was for no deep-seated Freudian reason, but merely my way of having a joke at my mother's expense. On one occasion, I was sitting in a railway carriage with my mother, who was speaking to the lady opposite. (People spoke to strangers on trains in those days.) Nora told her that Jack had been stationed up north for the past year but would be coming home soon.

'So you'll be pleased to see your Daddy then?' asked the woman.

'I haven't got a Daddy,' I replied.

'Oh, I am sorry,' said the woman (turning to Nora), 'but I thought you said . . .'

'Michael, now don't be silly, of course you have,' said a flustered Nora.

'No, I haven't. Jack's not my Daddy,' I said.

The woman, clearly wishing she hadn't started the whole thing off, returned to her library book.

'I was only joking,' I told Nora, as we made our way down the station platform.

'You love making a fool of me in public,' she said, which became one of her catchphrases.

And it wasn't just in front of Nora that I denied my father's existence. After the war, when we lived in a large Victorian house in Sydenham, I was at it again, though this time in front of Jack, just back from his desk job with the R.A.F. One Saturday morning, Jack accompanied Nora, Barry and me to the local butchers.

'Good morning, Mrs Whitehall, and this must be Mr Whitehall. I've heard all about you from Mrs Whitehall,' said the butcher, and turning to me. 'You must be pleased to have your Daddy home, Michael.'

Before Jack could reply, I cut in with: 'But *he's* not my Daddy.'

'Oh, I'm sorry,' said the bemused butcher, 'I just assumed . . .'

'Don't be silly Michael,' said Nora. 'Of course he is.'

'I'm not being silly Mummy, just truthful.'

'Right, Mrs Whitehall, what would you like? I've got some lovely pork belly today.'

'Why do you say all those things?' said Nora as we walked home.

'Because I think that butcher is really boring and very nosey.'

'I agree,' said Barry.

One of Nora's little quirks of paranoia was her daily and seemingly endless worry of being 'fobbed off' by shopkeepers of all persuasions. My instructions, when doing the shopping for her, always came with dire warnings of not being talked into accepting inferior goods.

At the butchers, everything had to be English: 'Don't let them fob you off with New Zealand lamb,' she'd say. ('New Zealand lamb couldn't possibly be fresh – do you realize how far away New Zealand is?') And of course the ham had to be York, the steak Scotch, the liver calves and the sausages pork (beef sausages were very common). She was always on the lookout for horse lurking on the shelves, although, as far as I can remember, none ever slipped through her tightly meshed net.

She was always very suspicious of fish, never believing it was entirely fresh (except if we were on a seaside holiday); but on our rare forays to the fishmongers, smoked salmon had to be Scotch and haddock, a favourite of hers, 'finnen'.

She had great brand loyalty. No baked bean ever crossed our plate unless it was from Heinz; no cereal unless it came from Kellogg's; and the only people who knew how to make butter properly were the Danes.

'Those eggs don't look very fresh,' she said to Jack one day when we were out shopping.

I asked Jack how could she tell that they weren't fresh just by looking at the shells.

'You know your mother,' he replied. 'Once she gets something into her head . . .'

Nora ran her life on keeping-up-appearances principles. By now we had moved up a rung and were living in a semi-detached house in Beckenham. At least I was able to tell my friends at school that I lived in Kent, even though a ten-minute walk would have landed me up in Penge.

When the doorbell rang (chimes rather than a bell, one of her few mistakes on the class front), the net curtains (another one) would twitch and she would move at enormous speed through the ground-floor rooms, clearing all surfaces of anything that might suggest that someone actually lived in the house. Books, papers, cups, saucers, all were shoved into cupboards; the television set, when we eventually could afford one, was wheeled behind a curtain. She would then carry out a quick check that the cloakroom loo seat was down and the bowl flushed, before rushing breathlessly to the front door. We tended not to have callers – more often than not, it would be the postman or the milkman – and certainly our neighbours wouldn't have dreamed of ringing the door-bell without prior appointment.

The local Catholic priest, Father Byrne, usually called a couple of times a year, again always by appointment. His arrival would be preceded by a top-to-bottom clean of the house on an industrial scale, with day-and-night vacuuming, polishing and dusting, and the removal of virtually the entire surface contents of the living rooms into the already overfilled cupboards and drawers. My mother would then lay on tea for Father Byrne. No ordinary tea was this, but a mélange of sandwiches, cakes and home-made scones, and a range of cake stands, slicers, trolleys, dessert knives and forks would appear from some little-used dresser, only to be returned after his visit and not seen again until his next appearance.

We had a very unreliable Pekinese dog called Candy, or to give him his full pedigree name Foxgrove Candy Floss. Candy was normally fairly even-tempered but when anywhere near food, especially any kind of meat product, he would turn into a wild beast. Perhaps he was traumatized by having a bitch's name. During one of Father Byrne's visits, Candy managed to get hold of a couple of meat-paste sandwiches which had fallen off the trolley. While Nora was in the kitchen putting together a selection of assorted fancies, Father Byrne approached Candy's basket to give him a stroke. Thinking that the priest was trying to snatch his sandwich, Candy leaped out of his basket and attached himself to Father Byrne's hand. On hearing the pandemonium in the drawing room, Nora rushed from the kitchen and grabbed hold of Candy, who promptly turned on her and stuck his teeth into her arm. Barry and I, who had been upstairs awaiting Nora's call to tea, managed to sort out the mayhem, although sadly it marked the last of Father Byrne's visits.

Nora, however, continued to be a regular worshipper at St Osmund's Church in Beckenham. Every Sunday we were all expected to attend the 11 a.m. Mass; this included Jack even though he was C of E. No question of course of our ever setting foot inside a C of E church, which Nora would have equated with a mosque or synagogue. A regular at St Osmund's was an Old Amplefordian financial adviser called Gerard Ussher-Smith. Ussher-Smith had looked after my parents' financial affairs, in so much as they had any, for years; and although he never did anything dishonest – or not that they noticed – there was the whiff of something dodgy about him.

'I think he's a crook,' said Barry. 'He asked me how much I had in my Post Office savings book the other day. I didn't tell him.'

I probably would have told him, had I not spent all my pocket money before it ever got near a savings book.

But as far as Nora was concerned, and Jack usually concurred, Ussher-Smith was a Catholic, so he must be OK.

Years later when I bought my first house in Barnes he came back into my life. He'd heard from Nora that I'd inherited some money from Ernest and offered to invest it for me. I would provide finance for one of his clients by way of a private mortgage on his house, all risk-free of course, and I would receive a much higher rate of interest than I'd get elsewhere. The paperwork looked fine to me – these were the bad days of unregulated financial advisers – so I handed over the five thousand pounds, a tidy sum in the 1960s, and waited for the interest to roll in. I had, of course, already taken predictable family advice.

'I'd tell him to fuck off,' said Barry.

'He told me he was doing some financial work for the monks at Ampleforth,' said Nora. '*They* certainly wouldn't get involved with someone who wasn't completely honest.'

In any case the interest cheques came in at the end of each month, and I had the security of a mortgage on a nice semi-detached house in Banstead, owned by a Mr Pritchard. Then, as Barry had predicted, the cheques stopped. I called Ussher-Smith, who assured me that everything was fine. A month passed and, after a couple of telephone calls, he became more aggressive.

'I told you you'll get the money. This is a very good investment from your point of view, so don't be greedy,' he ranted.

And then one day his telephone wasn't answered, and I discovered that he'd done a runner.

'I did warn you,' said Barry.

A few days later I had a telephone call from Mr Pritchard, telling me that he had a mortgage on my house and was going to have to call in the money as he had had no interest payments from me and that his financial adviser had disappeared. Mr Pritchard reacted badly to the news that I had a similar arrangement on his house. We met up and discovered that our so-called mortgages were valueless, and that Ussher-Smith had stolen our money. It turned out that he'd pulled the same trick on dozens of other unsuspecting investors. The police eventually caught up with him, and he did a couple of years in an open prison somewhere. I managed to track him down after his release and demanded the return of my five thousand pounds, but he refused to speak to me. I subsequently received a letter from his solicitors, accusing me of harassment. Nora said she felt sorry for him because his wife had been very ill, and he was probably using the money to fund her medical bills.

'Bollocks!' said Barry.

Another St Osmund's habitué was a young Pole, in his early twenties, who had been introduced to Nora by Father Byrne. His name was Eugene Voyack and, according to Father Byrne, had 'tragically lost his family during the war'. Nora took a great fancy to Eugene: she thought he was very attractive and courteous. He became a regular visitor to our house until one day Nora announced that he was coming to live with us. I heard Jack and Nora having various heated conversations about Eugene's permanent presence in the house. His whole background sounded melodramatic and, although always very charming to Nora, Jack thought there was something not quite right about him. Nevertheless, Nora would not be swayed from having this young man in the house, and within a few weeks started talking about adoption. This was a very different proposition. Eugene coming to stay for a few weeks was OK, but becoming our new brother, no way.

And then one day Eugene arrived from a trip to the West End with a present for me – a very impressive-looking gold watch, engraved on the back: 'TO BROTHER MICHAEL FROM EUGENE'. Jack and Barry thought that this was very definitely jumping the gun, while Nora thought it sweet. I, on the other hand, liked the watch very much. Barry was annoyed that he had been given only a rather dull book, similarly inscribed, but then he had been quite frosty to Eugene from the outset, suspecting that he might have some kind of hidden agenda.

A week or so later my watch stopped and Eugene took it to the West End to have it repaired. That evening I was disappointed to hear that it would be at least a week before I got it back. The following evening Eugene offered to read me a bedtime story (I must have been eight or nine at the time), and got into bed with me. The

following evening he read to me again and then
introduced me to a game called Lost Property. This
involved Eugene fumbling around my pyjama bottoms
looking for 'lost property' and finding it between my legs.
I mentioned this to Nora the following morning.
Needless to say, she was sure I was making the whole
thing up. Barry was less sure. That evening Eugene came
into my room with a copy of Enid Blyton's *Five Go Off
in a Caravan*, and before long we were into another round
of Lost Property. What should I do? I knew if I told my
father that would be the end of Eugene, but he still had
my watch and I really wanted it back. So I decided to put
up with a few more sessions of Eugene's little game. The
next evening, just as it was reaching its finale, the
bedroom cupboard door burst open and Barry sprang
out.

'Get out of my brother's bed, Eugene! I'm going to get
Mummy and Daddy.'

Nora was far too embarrassed to get involved, but Jack
ordered Eugene down to the sitting room. Moments later
Eugene was on the front doorstep with his suitcase. I
never saw him again, nor my watch for that matter. 'It
was fake gold anyway,' said Barry.

I'm not sure whether Barry ever quite forgave me for
being born. He was three years older than me and,
although we had the same parents, he seemed to be from
a different planet. We didn't look remotely alike: he was
tall and thin with curly black hair; I was podgy with a

cowlick of brown hair. He was deadpan to the point of being almost mute; I was a chatterbox. When an early school report mentioned that my meagre achievements were 'entirely spoilt by bastic buffoonery', Jack and Nora rushed to the dictionary. But they had no success in tracking down the word 'bastic' and assumed the teacher had made the word up, although, they agreed, it sounded like me. Barry, however, was neither bastic nor a buffoon. He took life and himself very seriously. 'I do wish you boys would get on better,' Nora pleaded and carried on pleading until the day she died. But it never really happened. After leaving school and doing National Service in the RAF, Barry joined the BBC and worked through a series of responsible jobs, ending his career as Head of Resources, World Service. This seemed to involve budgeting and approving various items needed by the BBC's far-flung outposts, such as a new radio mast for the Solomon Islands Broadcasting Company or refurbishing the hospitality area of their Greenland facility off Baffin Bay. A former Controller of the BBC's World Service once told me that Barry had overrun a meeting of heads of department by more than an hour by insisting that everyone around the table should have a copy of a proposal for a new toilet block attached to a facility in Tasmania. He then discussed in considerable detail the various financial options available to them. We would have happily nodded this through as a written request, said the former Controller, but Barry insisted on giving us every nuance of the project, down to the last toilet-roll dispenser.

Barry, unlike me, was conscientious, responsible and utterly reliable. He joined the BBC in the engineering department and then moved over to radio and subsequently into personnel. He spent his entire life there, and after he retired became a magistrate, ending up as chairman of the magistrates in Oxford. We were never the closest of siblings: I think he thought I was a loose cannon and got away with murder. He never asked Jack or Nora for money, while I seemed to be permanently on the edge of a major financial crisis, having spent unnecessary sums of money on what Barry would call 'fripperies'. 'Surely you haven't bought *another* tie,' he'd say. 'I have only one tie. You must have at least fifty. Why do you need fifty ties?'

He wasn't remotely surprised that I failed in my attempts at becoming a journalist, solicitor and barrister, and thought I'd reached my level when I told him I was working for a theatrical agency. After I'd started my own agency and was at last making a bit of money, he came for lunch at my new house in Putney.

'How much did this place cost?' he asked, rather abruptly. 'A fair bit, I would have thought.'

I rounded the sum down quite substantially, not wishing to appear too extravagant. I knew my place.

'Christ, wherever did you get that kind of money from? Did you . . .' (I thought Barry was going to say steal) 'borrow it? I imagine you've got a huge mortgage. How much?'

'A lot, actually,' I replied.

'Will you be able to service it?' he asked.

'Well, I hope . . .'

'I don't have a mortgage,' said Barry. 'But, as you know, my house is much smaller than *this*.'

He emphasized the *this* in that accusatory tone he had acquired as a child: 'You've *broken* it, Michael.'

'Well, I just hope you haven't overstretched yourself *again*,' he said.

I remember rather resenting the *again*, as I'd made a nice profit on my previous two houses, enabling me to push the boat out a bit.

'And do you need five bedrooms?' he asked.

I wanted to say I needed the five bedrooms to accommodate my fifty ties.

Fortunately I never ended up in the Oxford Magistrates' Court, though I'm sure Barry would have given me a hard time. 'Oh for God's sake, Michael, what are you doing here?' he would have asked. 'Not speeding again? Send him down for twelve months. Next case.'

But he did sort Eugene out for me, for which I was always grateful. I just wish his timing had been better – I miss that watch.

My father by now was working for a company called Westcoat & Intrex selling frocks to big stores in London.

Occasionally, if he had lots of samples to show the following morning, he would bring the company's van home. This had a very tall body and was clearly designed for housing rails of clothes. It also had WESTCOAT & INTREX FASHIONS in large letters on both sides and at the back. As Nora had told the neighbours that Jack was a retired naval officer who did some part-time consultancy work for Harrods, the van was a bit of a giveaway. So she insisted on it being parked in the next street, away from prying eyes. Jack seemed to change his job fairly regularly. George Smith & Sons, furriers, also had a high-backed van, which made brief appearances in Foxgrove Avenue, as did that of a firm of glove-makers in Wembley.

One of Nora's habitual embarrassments – and there were many – was her constant fear of being overlooked: our front and back windows were always swathed in net curtaining. Our new home at 45 Foxgrove Avenue was particularly desirable as it had heavily frosted glass on all windows, behind which daily ablutions or undressing would take place. Nora felt especially exposed in gardens and our new back garden was no exception. Within weeks of our arrival, Jack, Barry and I were instructed to dig a large hole in the middle of the lawn to prevent her being overlooked while taking the sun. Sunbathing was not a wholly accurate description of what she thought she would be overlooked doing, as she never took off any of her clothes. On the contrary, she tended to put on extra ones. With her large straw hat, enormous sunglasses, scarf and stockings (bare legs wouldn't have done at all), very little flesh was on show for the neighbours to feast their eyes on.

Instead it was the hole itself that caused all the local interest. Over six feet in diameter and of similar depth, it took us weeks to dig, and resulted in Jack having spasmodic back pain for the rest of his life. Nora referred to it rather grandly as the 'sunbathing area', but in reality it was just a large and unsightly hole in the middle of the lawn. Steps were cut out at one side, and there was an attempt to give it a rockery effect; although, after Jack had carried tons of rock across the lawn, Nora decided they looked rather 'common', so they all had to be lugged back again. She was also worried that if she slipped on one of the makeshift steps, she would be gashed to death on the rocks below.

We spread liberal amounts of grass seed on the sides and base in an attempt to make it look less like a hole in the middle of the garden. Unfortunately, the seed didn't take as the sun never got to it. Indeed, this was the problem: the sun never got down there at all. Unfortunately the rain did, and Barry and I often had to bucket out the muddy water before putting up Nora's deckchair.

And then, quite suddenly, Nora decided that she didn't like sitting in the hole after all. It was cold, dark, damp and slippery, and she found the steps impossible to manage. So Jack filled it in over the next couple of weeks, doing further damage to his back. Nora gave up the idea of sunbathing altogether, making do with a seat on the patio, which was well protected from prying eyes by arbours, trellising and pergolas.

In order to give our garden a bit of style, now that the hole had been filled, Nora had Jack buy a dovecote; and in order to set off the effect, Jack was dispatched to Chislehurst to buy a pair of white doves. The doves were wired into the dovecote, as the man who sold them to Jack had advised, and two days later the wire was removed. The doves would now remain in the garden and return to the dovecote after they'd had a fly around the garden. Perfect. Nora thought they looked just the ticket. Unfortunately, they both flew off within an hour of the mesh being removed and were never seen again. Jack was sent back to Chislehurst, where he bought another pair. The man said it was most unusual.

'Perhaps they weren't meshed in for long enough,' he suggested.

Of course, the second pair of doves flew away too, and Jack had to make a third and final visit to Chislehurst, returning with a pair of doves that looked remarkably like the first pair. This pair did a runner with similar alacrity. Barry thought the man in Chislehurst had a very nice little earner going for him, and Nora decided that the dovecote looked fine without any doves; it avoided having all those unsightly bird droppings.

Jack was always wonderful at keeping up with all the non-existent Joneses in Nora's life. He was a sharp dresser and always neat and tidy. I used to love watching him shave in the morning with his shiny cutthroat razor, and then the smell of cologne when the job was done. His shoes were always beautifully polished, his cuff-links gold and gleaming, and his full head of hair brushed back over the forehead with a pair of white horn hairbrushes. He always looked far too elegant to be heading off in his van to try and sell ladies' dresses to the buyers of various large department stores in the West End. But he was a good salesman.

'The buyers feel sorry for Jack,' Nora once told me, 'they think he looks sad so they give him a big order. It's all an act, of course.'

I wish I'd got to know Jack better, but he was always a bit of a closed book and a man of few words. I remember his bone-dry sense of humour best of all. Shortly before he died of emphysema – he was only in his late fifties and a heavy smoker – we went to see a film at the Curzon cinema in Mayfair. As the exhaustive credits rolled out at the end of the film, one caught his eye: 'Production Accountant: Gerald Atwood'.

'Of course,' he said to me, 'of course, Gerald Atwood, Production Accountant. I should have guessed. The film had his name written all over it.'

2

A Little Learning

Nora's social aspirations were never fully realized after her marriage to Jack, although she continued to love him. 'He was a saint,' she would later say, 'but try living with one.' And yet it wasn't Jack's saintliness she disliked; it was his lack of class. Unfortunately, since her marriage to him, Nora found herself being dragged further and further back into the lower middle class from whence she had come. It might be too late for Jack and me now, she often thought, so let's give the boys a chance. The problem was how. A public school education would be a good start, but she knew little of that world and Jack, despite having been at Cranleigh for all of five minutes, knew even less. Nora had a phrase for it – 'à la carte' – which cropped up a lot in her conversation. There was very little in the way of 'à la carte' in Foxgrove Avenue, Beckenham. Nevertheless, on one of her weekly trips to the Bromley School of Art Nora met someone who fitted the bill perfectly.

Hermione Eggamanders reeked of class. The stylish wife of a portrait painter, Hermione was in Nora's life class at Bromley and, although Nora never had the courage to invite her back to Foxgrove Avenue (Hermione lived in a rambling rectory near Westerham), they had had tea together. At one of their teas, Nora broached the subject of public schools. To her delight it turned out that Hermione was a Catholic and her two half-brothers had been to a school called Ampleforth College. That did it for Nora: if the school was good enough for Hermione's brothers, even if they were only half-brothers, then it was certainly good enough for her sons. Before she discussed our education with Jack, however, she had to make further investigations.

Nora was disappointed to discover that Ampleforth was not only two hundred and twenty miles from London but was miles from the nearest town, being stuck in a valley on the edge of the North Yorkshire moors. She wrote off for a prospectus and received a charming letter from the headmaster, Father Paul Nevill, inviting her to come and visit the school. Despite the school's inconvenient location, she liked the idea of us being taught by Benedictine monks. There was, however, no question of Nora visiting the school before our arrival. For a start Jack and Nora had no transport, apart from Jack's Westcoat & Intrex van, which was wholly inappropriate. Not to mention the fact that the monks were probably very 'à la carte', and Nora couldn't risk letting

Jack loose on them. And then there was the question of fees. There was no way that Jack's income could cover two sets of boarding school fees, and Nora's paltry savings wouldn't even have covered the rail fares. So it was down to Worthing to see if Ernest would help.

'What's wrong with Whitgift in Croydon?' asked Ernest. 'Much cheaper, much nearer and C of E.'

Ernest was not keen on Catholics, and had still not forgiven Jack for marrying one. He'd also never heard of this strange school Nora had come up with. So when he was told that the school was run by Benedictine monks all the wrong bells started ringing.

'Do you really want to send the boys to a school you know nothing about, apart from the fact that it's in the wilds of the Yorkshire moors and run by a bloody sect of monks?'

As the idea was for Ernest to pay the fees, or at least most of them, Nora went through the motions of 'considering' Whitgift, which meant she had to go and see it. Unsurprisingly, it was everything she didn't want; it wasn't Catholic, and certainly in no way 'à la carte'. And it was in Croydon. Ernest finally succumbed to Nora's advances: she had great charm when she wanted to use it and Ernest probably admired her determination, even if he didn't particularly agree with it. So Barry headed off for Gilling Castle, the Ampleforth prep school, and two years later, I followed him there.

King's Cross Station in the 1950s was a pretty austere location for a nine-year-old's first encounter with a group of monks. I had not been to see the school beforehand, and Jack and Nora had visited it only once during Barry's two years there. Nevertheless, by the time the train had reached Peterborough, I had already made friends with a couple of other tearful new boys, and by Grantham we were all exchanging jokes. Changing trains at York, we arrived at Gilling East Station at dusk and transferred on to a bus which took us up the hill, where we were met by a group of black-habited monks or 'crows'. Crows also circled the castle, giving it more than a passing resemblance to Colditz.

As I fell asleep in the dormitory a few hours later, I felt a very long way away from Nora and Jack in Foxgrove Avenue. As the days went by I continued to feel homesick and decided to do what all self-respecting children reluctantly sent away to boarding school do: I would run away.

I surprised myself at the speed with which I formulated a plan and put it into action. I had held back some of the pocket money Jack had given me at King's Cross Station, which was supposed to be handed over to the housemaster, Father Henry, on arrival. Moreover, I had worked out the timings of the Reliant Bus Company's service from Gilling to York, and found out from Matron, whose parents also lived in London, the times of the trains from York to King's Cross. Escaping from Colditz seemed to present few problems to an optimistic young nine-year-old. 'Free time', a two-hour period between prep and bed, seemed to having running away written all over it.

I caught the bus at the bottom of the hill to York Station just in time for the 8 p.m. train to London.

'I'd like a single to King's Cross, please,' I asked the man in the ticket office.

'I'm sorry,' he said, 'the King's Cross train has just left.'

'But it can't have, it's only seven-thirty,' I said.

'Sorry son, it's five past eight. The next one's at seven-thirty tomorrow morning.'

My watch had stopped. Nora had bought me a Timex as a going-away-to-school present, but of course it needed winding every day. (If only I had had Eugene's gold watch, I might have caught the train.) In planning my escape, I had forgotten to wind the Timex. I was despondent. What should I do now? By 8.30 p.m. my disappearance would be discovered.

I walked straight into the Royal Station Hotel.

'I'd like a single room for the night, please,' I asked confidently. Having not bought my ticket yet, I thought I might have just enough money for a room.

After what seemed like an interminable wait, the receptionist said, 'If you go and sit over there, sir, we'll get your room ready. It won't be a moment.'

As I sat in the corner, trying to make sense of the business pages of the *Yorkshire Post*, I should have known the game was up. Suddenly, the swing doors swooshed open, and there stood Father Henry.

On the way back to school, Father Henry told me that he had had a telephone call from the hotel manager; and that if I was planning any more escapes, it would probably be wise not to wear my Gilling Castle blazer and give more attention to the whole matter of disguise. Most importantly, I should keep an accurate timepiece to hand.

My parents were informed, and Nora wrote me a letter stating how embarrassing it had been for her having Father Henry on the telephone – and how he was much more 'à la carte' than she had previously thought.

Gilling Castle, which catered for eight- to twelve-year-old boys, was run by Father Hilary Barton. He was a scary figure, with more than a passing resemblance to Heinrich Himmler and probably much in common with him when it came to corporal punishment. Before lunch every day, miscreants would line up outside the book room where Father Hilary, in full habit, would stand holding a ferule – a flat black ruler with a wide end, which some disciple of the Marquis de Sade had invented for the express purpose of beating children. Two on each hand for a minor offence: late for class, talking in class or just mucking about (my speciality). Three or four would be given for greater misdemeanours: being rude to Matron or cheating in class. After the beating, we would rush to the washrooms and lay our hot, stinging hands – the corners below the thumbs were always the most painful – in a basin of cold water until the lunch bell rang.

I can still remember how cold the knife and fork felt in my hands as I savoured the finer points of spam fritters. For the worst offences, such as missing mass or, worse still, missing games (another speciality of mine), an evening visit, appropriately dressed, to Father Hilary's study was called for. After a brief lecture on the wages of sin – the dressing gown having been taken off and the winceyette pyjama bottoms dropped to the floor (mine not his) – it was 'six of the best' with the slipper. Giving a boy a good slippering was a more difficult proposition than the traditional caning (the ferule wasn't suitable for the bottom): the slipper was a more pliable implement, requiring a stronger and straighter aim, which Father Hilary had perfected over many a year of nocturnal thrashing. The slipper, black and sleek, matching the rest of his outfit, was at least an eleven-and-a-half, whereas Father Hilary, a relatively small man, looked as if he wore a size eight. As far as I know, he used this pair only for slippering and, presumably, had a dress pair for personal use. Once, when I was in a particularly obnoxious mood, I managed to get the slipper out of his hand in mid-flow, but this offered me only temporary respite.

'Now don't be silly, Whitehall,' he said. 'Give it back.'

'Sorry, sir, but it hurts,' I replied.

For one moment I thought he might respond with, 'It hurts me more than it does you', but in fact he just glowered at me, rimless glasses gleaming on the end of his thin red nose.

'I'm going to have to give you an extra six.'

Did these evening experiences leave me mentally and physically scarred for life? Well, not really. Obviously, I thought that most of my punishments were unfair, which, in most cases, they weren't. It was all part of the game, and I remember thanking Father Hilary before returning to my dormitory. Nora would certainly have thought it was all for the best.

'You really must stop fooling around all the time, dear,' she would say. 'Poor Father Hilary, I'm sure the last thing he wants to do in the evenings is beat you boys.'

I was never sure about that.

Sexual abuse was supposed to be rife within the Catholic teaching community in those days, but the nearest I came to it was fending off another Gilling monk, Father Drostan, during his nocturnal sorties into the dormitories. Although the North Yorkshire moors are not renowned for their tropical climate, on supposedly warm summer nights Father Drostan would regularly invite us to his room for what he invitingly referred to as 'a rub down with a dry towel'. Nothing much happened, but, nevertheless, Catholic guilt came into play – even at that age. What Father Drostan was or wasn't doing just didn't seem right. So one night, Whitehall, Rothwell and Burn, headed for Father Hilary's study, three winceyette-clad boys on a mission.

'May we have a word, sir?' I said, having been elected spokesman.

'Come in and sit down,' said Father Hilary. 'Trouble sleeping?'

'Well . . . not really, sir . . . actually sir . . . we wanted to tell you about Father Drostan.'

I then ran over the regular scenario involving the removal of dressing gowns, slippers and pyjamas, and the appearance of Father Drostan's considerable range of bath towels. Father Hilary thanked us for our visit and bade us goodnight.

Father Drostan failed to appear at morning assembly and, indeed, was never seen at the school again. There was a rumour that deviant monks were sent to a special community on the north coast of Scotland where impure thoughts were beaten out of them.

Rothwell was my best friend at Gilling. I called him 'Rothwell' because, in those days, Christian names were never used at school either by teachers or pupils; even sympathetic figures such as matrons stuck to surnames. In the holidays it was difficult to slide into Christian names: 'Rothwell' was 'Rothwell', not 'Christopher'. (I'm now not quite sure whether that *was* his name.) He certainly wouldn't have dreamed of calling me 'Michael'.

Rothwell invited me to stay with his family at Morebath Manor near Tiverton in Devon. Nora spent days packing my case and giving me various tips about what to do when staying in stately homes. Tipping the staff, dressing for dinner (she packed so many changes of clothes that I ended up taking a large trunk), putting the lavatory seat down after use and using the right cutlery. One thing she failed to mention, however, resulted in a horrendous *faux pas* at the breakfast table.

First down for breakfast, I'd waited patiently for Mrs Rothwell to put a plate of bacon and eggs in front of me, as Nora did in Foxgrove Avenue. When she hadn't appeared, I helped myself to a slice of toast from the table. When she finally arrived with Major Rothwell, Rothwell and his sister, they headed straight for the sideboard and started producing a mouth-watering array of food from a range of silver dishes.

'Not having the cooked breakfast, eh?' asked Major Rothwell. 'Plenty here, old boy – eggs, bacon, tomato, sausages, mushrooms, the lot.'

'No thank you sir,' I lied, 'I'm fine with toast.'

Of course I wasn't fine with the toast – I was starving – but it was too late.

When I told Nora what had happened, she went into shock. All that scrimping and saving, and I didn't know about silver dishes on sideboards.

'Was there k-kedgeree?' she asked hesitantly.

Poor Nora, she so wanted to be a million miles away from Foxgrove Avenue.

Now it was Rothwell's turn to stay with us. Arriving at breakfast at the same time as Jack, there was a brief moment of silent embarrassment as Nora led him across to the sideboard, which usually sat in the hall with a plant on it.

'Will you have a cooked breakfast?' asked my mother.

'Yes, please,' interjected Jack.

'Well, help yourself,' replied Nora.

Jack got up and made for the kitchen.

'Where are you going?'

'To help myself.'

'But it's in the usual place,' said Nora, throwing her eyes towards the sideboard.

Jack ambled over to where Rothwell was helping himself.

'Nora,' said Jack, 'why have you put bacon in your jewellery box?'

Nora fixed Jack with one of her not inconsiderable death stares.

'And what are these eggs doing in my silver cigarette box?'

All the effort of collecting, polishing and cleaning a selection of silver boxes for breakfast had been for nothing. Jack had let her down yet again. Rothwell seemed to be unfazed by the whole event.

Later in the holidays, Nora arranged for Mrs Eggamanders's daughter Angela to join us at a dinner dance at the Selsdon Park Hotel. This was a rare event in Jack and Nora's normally barren social calendar, but now that Jack had started playing golf, Nora thought it was time the family started going out more.

Angela was twelve, a year or so older than me, and quite pretty in a tall, lanky kind of way. In fact, she was several inches taller than me, and her blossoming bosom caused me some embarrassment during the slower dances. Angela's parents seemed very charming although not remotely posh, as Nora had led us all to believe. Mr Eggamanders, or Brian, turned out to be an insurance salesman and not a portrait painter.

As Angela and I found ourselves alone at the table towards the end of the evening, she slid her hand on to my knee, which sent me into shock. I had not yet had any kind of physical experience of the opposite sex and indeed was keen to avoid the whole thing for the time being. Well, at least until I'd got the hang of it all a bit better. Jack and Nora were no help and always veered away from the subject when I tried to broach it. Nora was still 'dressing' the nudes she painted at Bromley School of Art before bringing them home, 'just in case Michael sees them'. Sexual encounters were thin on the ground as I moved between an all-male community on the Yorkshire moors to a sexually repressed Catholic family in the London suburbs. I chatted to Angela between dances, but couldn't find much common ground apart from the fact that we loathed these kinds of evenings and both had fathers who were salesmen. We made some very vague plans to meet again and, when we said goodbye, Angela gave me a 'tongue kiss', to which I responded rather inexpertly as I had just put a Fox's Glacier Mint into my mouth and was frightened of swallowing it.

The evening at Selsdon Park was not repeated. Brian Eggamanders spent most of the evening trying to sell Jack life insurance; Hermione had too much to drink; and Nora never recovered from accidentally referring to the ladies' lavatory as the 'toilet'. I found the whole evening particularly stressful: I wish I'd been able to find a topic of conversation with Angela that might have been of any interest to either of us. I never saw her again.

Once I had left Gilling, I moved on to Ampleforth. My French master there was Basil Hume, who subsequently became Abbot of Ampleforth and later Cardinal Archbishop of Westminster. Father Basil was, in my view, the ultimate monk: a genuinely holy man with a wonderful sense of humour. Arriving to take a French lesson, he climbed up to the large wooden desk, passing on the step a brown plastic object (at the time known only to me as a 'Dirty Fido'). On a recent trip to the joke shop in York, I had bought this object hoping that it might get me a cheap laugh at school, and it was making its first appearance at the foot of Father Basil's desk.

Having set us a passage to translate, Father Basil rose from the desk. Out of the corner of my eye, I spotted him bending down to pick up the Dirty Fido. He then walked across the classroom and, as he reached my desk, placed it in front of me.

'Yours, I think, Whitehall,' he said.

Before I had a chance to deny it he went on, 'Very amusing. What the French call *merde*.' Father Basil's mother was French, so he had a useful command of the French colloquial.

At the end of the class, as we filed out into the corridor, I said, 'Sir, why did you think this had anything to do with me?'

'As I walked into the classroom I saw it perched on the step of the desk and a heavenly shaft of light blazed down on to your head, and I thought "Whitehall".'

'Sorry, sir,' I replied.

He smiled. 'I'm afraid it's confiscated. Pick it up at the end of term. I'm sure you'll get good value out of it during the holidays.'

Twenty years later, Ampleforth organized a reception for the new Archbishop in London and invited old boys of the school to attend. Although I wasn't a particularly dedicated old boy, I thought this was a special occasion that I shouldn't miss. A large number of people were milling round Father Basil, whom I had not seen since leaving school, so I had to wait my turn. I noticed that everybody was kneeling and kissing his ring; I made a note not to miss out on this important bit of ritual. Finally, I reached the head of the queue and went down on one knee and kissed his hand.

'I hope you are not leaving that Dirty Fido down there, Michael,' he said.

★　★　★

' ''Yours, I think, Whitehall'' '

Jack and Nora made their first visit to Ampleforth for the Exhibition weekend (a prize-giving event that took place during the summer term), which for them required organization akin to that of the D-day landings. First, there was the transport. We didn't have a car, well certainly not one in which Nora would be seen dead within a hundred-mile radius of the school. Jack had recently bought a second-hand Ford Popular, but it was extremely unreliable and broke down at the slightest excuse. Cold weather, hot weather, rain and shine were all enemies of the Ford Popular; the thought of Nora helping Jack to jump-start the car in front of five hundred sets of parents, boys and monks was the stuff of nightmares for her. She had insisted that Jack become a member of the AA, mainly because she liked being saluted by the patrolmen. But even an AA-assisted breakdown en route to Yorkshire would have been catastrophic. What if the Rothwells had driven past in their sleek Alvis and had spotted Jack with his head under the bonnet? There was, of course, the Westcoat & Intrex van, which was the height of reliability, but for obvious reasons that wouldn't do. Nora would rather have slashed her wrists in front of the headmaster than step out of a van in the school car park. So it was the train from King's Cross to York, and a taxi thereafter.

And then there was accommodation. Financial restraints and the worry that Jack might use the wrong cutlery prohibited their staying at any of the better local hotels. The Black Swan at Helmsley or the Worseley

Arms at Hovingham were also overpriced, Nora thought, unlike Mrs Dale's B&B in Ampleforth village. Mrs Dale was a Katie Johnson look-alike (think Mrs Wilberforce in *The Ladykillers*), who, in addition to offering B&B facilities to college parents on limited budgets, also provided their offspring with illicit mid-week teas during which one was allowed to smoke and drink alcohol. She served a mean double-poached egg on toast and a decent range of home-made scones; we provided the beer and cigarettes. At the time I was experimenting with various exotic brands of cigarette: Abdulla Turkish Ovals, Black Russian Sobranie and Gitanes (untipped). Although we were in Mrs Dale's cottage for only a couple of hours, I was usually able to smoke at least five cigarettes during that time. But Mrs Dale was the height of discretion and would never let on that I visited her once a fortnight for smoking orgies. As far as Jack and Nora were concerned she had a nice clean guest bedroom, which suited them fine, and the cottage was well netted from prying eyes. Its only drawback was the lack of an indoor lavatory.

Next on Nora's agenda was what to wear. Discussions would start at the beginning of the year, and by early summer she had spent the same amount of time Scott must have taken on preparations for his Antarctic expedition. Hats were bought and then returned for being too common, shoes were too tarty, dresses too short, necklines too low.

'Father Paul won't want to see my bosom hanging out all over him,' Nora would say.

'Why not?' Jack would reply.

Jack's wardrobe was a more modest affair: blue blazer, grey flannels and his Old Cranleighan tie.

'I'm amazed you're wearing that tie,' Nora would tell him. 'You were only at Cranleigh for one term. What would you say if you bumped into a *real* Old Boy?'

Jack had been sent to Cranleigh despite his father's reservations about boarding schools, because his brother Cyril was there and doing very well. Sadly, Jack had a miserable time: he was homesick and bullied, and generally hopeless. So he left at the end of his first term and went to Whitgift instead.

With transport, accommodation and wardrobe under control, it was time for Nora to turn her attention to the question of friends. The problem was that she didn't have many. She didn't know any of my friends' parents personally, although she had spoken to the Rothwells on the telephone. In truth, she felt exposed appearing at the Exhibition weekend with only Jack in tow. So she asked Eileen Growsky, whom she had met at St Osmund's. Eileen was Polish, and her husband, a count, had left her for a much younger woman early in their marriage. Jack was never shy in telling Nora that counts were two a penny in Poland, but Nora thought Eileen racy and interesting with her fondness for vodka and French cigarettes, and the right kind of person to join her for the Ampleforth weekend.

Mrs Dale was unable to accommodate Eileen but arranged for her to stay with a neighbour. On the Friday evening, the Whitehall party was deposited outside her cottage by a taxi from York. There was an awkward moment for Jack when, shortly after arriving, he visited the outdoor lavatory. He placed himself on the wooden seat, and was quickly in action when he realized too late that there was nothing between him and the ground. What he did not know was that Mrs Dale's husband, Stanley, was behind the privy, having just removed the pan through the rear hatch, in order to clean it in readiness for the new guests. Stanley reported the incident to his wife, who made the mistake of apologizing to Nora. Anything to do with lavatories was not an area Nora enjoyed visiting: indeed visiting them at all was traumatic for her, especially other people's lavatories. Windows were flung open, even in the most Arctic weather, to disguise any giveaway odours. A non-flushing pan, with the resultant floater, was her ultimate nightmare, and it was a wonder she ever visited a lavatory at all. She would rather have crouched in a field than use the Dales' privy. It was a good thing their neighbours had indoor facilities.

On the Saturday morning, as the cars came down the drive and parked in front of the school, the boys would spot their parents and greet them. After half an hour of meeting and greeting, I was still standing on my own awaiting Jack and Nora's arrival. Where were they? The village was only ten minutes from the school. They knew they had to be at the school by midday. Finally, they came into view, looking hot, flustered, dishevelled and on foot.

As we entered the school theatre, just as the doors were closing and the headmaster was about to make his speech, Jack explained that Stanley had talked them out of ordering a taxi and offered to drive them.

'Why your father agreed I simply cannot imagine,' said Nora. 'First of all the car wouldn't start, so Mr Dale had to get a neighbour to jump-start it. We drove out of the village and he stopped at the garage to get petrol, which took hours. Then, of course, the car wouldn't restart, so we had to go through the whole process again.'

'Also the car was filthy, and I got oil on my dress,' said Eileen.

'Anyway, by the time we got to the top of the drive, it was making so much smoke that your mother thought we'd better walk down the drive. Still it was nice of him to offer,' said Jack.

'Nice for him maybe. I can't believe you said yes,' said Nora. 'Eileen, that oil on your skirt looks terrible.'

The rest of the weekend passed uneventfully. Eileen met some Polish friends who invited her to join them for dinner at the Black Swan in Helmsley.

'Why don't we ever meet people like that, Jack?' said Nora. 'Eileen said she had met them at the opera last month. We never go to the opera; we never go anywhere. Why couldn't you come home one evening with a pair of opera tickets?'

'But you don't like the opera.'

'That's got nothing to do with it.'

While at Ampleforth, I played the drums in the school orchestra – or the timpani to give them their grander Latin name. Being in charge of the whole percussion department, I was also expected to play the tambourine, the triangle, cymbals and various other bits of equipment requiring little or no skill. Not for me endless piano lessons in cold music rooms – a good bash on the drums satisfied all my musical aspirations. There was, however, one area of skill required when running a percussion section: the ability silently to count while surrounded by the booming, and in the case of the Ampleforth School Orchestra, often discordant, sounds coming from the rest of the players. I was positioned next to boy called Grant-Oxley who played the French horn really badly, seldom hitting the right note and having a remarkable facility for getting his instrument to backfire, particularly when playing at speed. There were of course some guest players in the orchestra with more control over their instruments. I remember that Piers Paul Read's mother played a particularly fine viola and there were several gifted monks among the violins. But to get back to the counting: if you are playing the violin in an orchestra, you generally find that you're scraping away most of the time and if you hit the odd wrong note, at the wrong time, nobody will notice, unless of course you are the soloist in a violin concerto, pieces the school orchestra tended to avoid. But, if you're playing the triangle and the triangle comes in after bar 135, 147 and 226 in the second movement of a Schubert symphony, and you've get Grant-Oxley making horrendous farting noises on his French horn in front of you, it's jolly difficult stuff. Hit the triangle at the wrong time and you're in an H. M. Bateman cartoon – the percussionist who hit his triangle on the wrong beat of a Schubert symphony. Small contribution – big responsibility.

I discovered later in life that actors have a similar problem. The leading actor with the major role is fine – *Macbeth*, *Hamlet*, *Hedda Gabler*, no problem. Word perfect, and anyway if you miss out the odd word or even line, who is going to notice other than some theatrical pedant? But what about the supporting actor with, in some cases, only one or two lines in the whole play? Standing in the wings, waiting for his big moment, having spent the past hour playing non-speaking towns-folk, soldiers and attendants.

I heard of an actor, fallen on hard times, who had accepted a tiny part in a touring production of a play. He had one line: 'The enemy's cannon are at the gates.'

He stood in the wings repeating the line over and over again. 'The enemy's cannon are at the gates. The enemy's cannon are at the gates.'

His moment came. He ran on to the stage. Behind him he heard a huge explosion. He turned to the actor next to him.

'What the fuck was that?' he shouted.

Sometimes a bit-part actor with only a line or two can cause havoc to the star's performance while appearing blameless himself. For example, instead of delivering the correct line to Lear, ' 'Tis true my lord he did,' the officer, a four-line part, says, ' 'Tis true my lord he didn't.' This, of course, throws the actor playing Lear into total confusion and instead of replying, 'Did I not fellow?' he says, 'Did I fellow?' and promptly forgets the rest of the speech. Kent then dries because he's been given the wrong line. Lear then says, 'This is a dull sight, are you not Kent?' By which time Kent has not only forgotten who he is, but the rest of his lines, and all thanks to the officer who walks off stage, squeaky clean, and leaves them to it.

Joking with people's lines is not, however, to be recommended; the joke can sometimes – like Grant-Oxley's French horn – backfire. The infamous actor-manager Donald Wolfit was touring in a production of *Henry V* and giving the company, especially the actors playing the supporting parts, a particularly rough ride. There is a scene in the play where a messenger hands the king a parchment, which he reads aloud. As the lines were written on the parchment, Wolfit never bothered to learn them and one night, the actor playing the messenger, aided by the stage management, handed Wolfit a blank parchment. He unfurled it, saw that it was blank, handed it back to the messenger and said, 'Read it to me, sirrah.'

As the only university interested in offering me a place was Hull – and this was in the late 1950s, when Hull was not what it is today – I decided to start earning a living. I went for an interview at the *Universe*, a weekly Catholic newspaper based off Chancery Lane, and got a job as a general reporter. Having run the school magazine at Ampleforth, I was at least able to cobble together a few stories, but the scope was limited and the high point of my week was reviewing films for the paper. Unfortunately, this tended to be a fairly pointless exercise as the reviews were published only if the films had some relevance to the Catholic Church – which ruled out virtually everything. I remember seeing a Fellini film called *Le Notti di Cabiria* because it was set in Rome, but it turned out to be about a Roman prostitute, so unsuitable for the *Universe*'s readership. I had a similar lack of success with *God's Little Acre*, which on release was being billed as 'the story no one dared to film until now . . . the most adult motion picture ever made'. I did, however, get my review of *The Maid of Lourdes* published. After six months of treading holy water, I decided it was time to move on. I was turned down as the assistant to the assistant film critic on the *Daily Telegraph*, where a wider range of titles would have been open to me, so I finally succumbed to Nora's pressure and joined Williams & James in South Square, Gray's Inn, as a solicitor's articled clerk.

Around this time Ernest died and left Jack some money, which financed a move from the suburban wastes of Beckenham to the Knightsbridge chic of 44 Pont Street. Nora loved Pont Street: it was handy for Harrods – even though she never went there – and within walking distance of the Brompton Oratory. I would set off each morning in my pinstripe suit, complete with rolled umbrella and bowler hat, to Williams & James, and follow round various partners doing their bidding. After I'd been there for a couple of months, my friend David Ryder, a lothario whom I greatly admired for the suave and relaxed way in which he handled girls, asked me if I would like to join him and his girlfriend for a weekend in Brighton.

'We'll leave on Saturday morning and go in the Bentley,' said David. 'Bring someone with you and I'll fix up a hotel for Saturday night.'

David had a sleek, green vintage Bentley which was quite an eye-catcher. The invitation seemed like fun, apart from one problem: 'Bring someone with you.' David had an address book full of young lovelies who would happily join him for a trip to Brighton in his flash car. I, on the other hand, had very limited resources in that department.

The following morning, as I was talking to the senior partner's secretary about a will I was trying to sort out, I caught the eye of Daphne, the office receptionist, who gave me a big beaming smile. Daphne bore more than a passing resemblance to Jayne Mansfield: she was a big girl in every way and looked as if she would fit easily into one of the Bentley's back seats. Over lunch, I discussed my dilemma with a fellow articled clerk, Brian Eastley-Hoare.

'Why don't you just ask her?'

'But I hardly know her. Apart from "good morning" and "goodnight", and a couple of brief conversations about the weather, I haven't really spoken to her. I don't even know where she lives.'

'Well ask her. To be honest, she's not quite my type and anyway I've got a girlfriend; but I would have thought she'd be perfect for a dirty weekend in Worthing.'

'Brighton, actually, and I hadn't really thought of it as a dirty weekend. In fact, I think the overnight bit might be a bridge too far for a first date.'

'Well, I'd just play it by ear. But get on with it; you've only got a couple of days and it'll be the weekend.'

So after lunch I chatted to Daphne over some letters she was stamping and, as she was in mid-lick, popped the question.

'D-do you have any w-weekend p-plans?' I stuttered.

'What, this weekend, do you mean?' she replied.

'Yes, well . . .'

'Well, I guess that depends on what you have in mind,' she giggled, and her mountainous breasts heaved provocatively. 'Nothing naughty, I hope?'

What a great start, I thought. I explained everything: Brighton, David and his girlfriend, the Bentley, but left out the overnight bit for the time being.

'I'd love to. Where do you want me?' she asked. This was going even better than I could have imagined.

'Have you finished that will?' the senior partner bellowed from his office door. 'Can we get on with some work, Whitehall? And Daphne, if you've finished stamping those letters, will you make me some coffee?'

I managed to have a quick word with Daphne as she put on her raincoat. I thought she looked more like Gina Lollobrigida in the raincoat than Jayne Mansfield – or maybe even Sophia Loren.

'I live in Sydenham, actually, but I can get up to London. Where did you say? Punt Street?'

'I'll give you directions tomorrow.'

'I'll bring an overnight bag, you know, just in case. Night, night.' And off she glided.

'Wow,' said Brian, 'you see, I told you.'

'I'm still not sure about the overnight bit.'

'Take a condom, just in case.'

On my way home I worried about actually buying the condoms. The chemist on Brompton Road was really nosey, and I didn't want him telling Nora what I was up to. There was a long queue, which included a woman who lived in the flat opposite us. Once she had left I shot up to the counter.

'One packet of condoms, please,' I whispered. The woman behind me looked very like a friend of Nora's from the Brompton Oratory.

'Yes, any preference? I've got Trojans, Romeos, just one six pack left of the Peacocks and, of course, the standard Durex.' I sensed a tut from the lady behind me who I was now convinced was Nora's friend.

'Actually, they are not for me. They're for a friend who's here on holiday from Italy.'

'So?' said the chemist.

'I'll take just one standard Durex.'

'Six pack or twelve?'

'Oh, I really only need one. W-well, my friend does.'

'They only come in sixes or twelves.' The woman behind was beginning to get agitated.

'Right, six please.'

'You might need six with Daphne,' Brian said the following morning. 'She looks like a real goer.'

It was now Friday morning and most of the partners were heading off to the country. The senior partner always wore a grey suit (three-piece, of course) on a Friday to indicate the approaching weekend, but the articled clerks had to stick to dark pinstripe.

'Good night, Whitehall,' he said as I was fine-tuning the following morning's arrangements with Daphne.

'Good night, Daphne,' he called, 'nice weekend to you both.'

Little did he know.

The following morning Jack and Nora headed off to Dorking to have lunch with Eileen, and David Ryder, girlfriend and Bentley arrived outside the flat at eleven o'clock.

'Perfect day for it, Michael,' he said. 'All packed?'

I had, in fact, packed a very small suitcase, the main contents of which, apart from a sponge bag containing the six-pack Durex, was a new pair of rather dashing white pyjamas. I'd briefly thought about a silk cravat, but thought I might frighten Daphne off if I looked too much like Noël Coward.

'What time is your girlfriend appearing?' David asked.

Girlfriend, yes that sounded good, I thought.

'Any time now,' I said glancing at my watch. I'd asked Daphne to be here at 10.45 and it was now 11.15. By 11.30 David was getting restless, and I was beginning to get nervous.

'Does she have your telephone number?' he asked.

'Yes. She's probably running late. She's coming from Syd . . .'

The telephone rang.

'Hello,' I said.

'Is your name Whitehall?'

'Who is speaking?'

'Is your name Whitehall, I said?' The voice sounded rough and angry.

'Yes. Who is this?'

'My name's Dean Streeter. I'm Daphne's boyfriend. I believe you've asked Daphne down to Brighton for the weekend?'

'Is it Daphne?' whispered David. 'Is she on her way?'

'W–well, yes, well, out for the day.'

'Look, mate, I don't care whether it's for the day or the night, or for whatever you've got in mind. She's not going anywhere, and if you ever suggest taking her out again, I'll come up to fucking Cunt Street, or whatever it's called, and break both your fucking legs. Goddit?'

'Yes, I see. So Daphne can't make it then. What a . . .'

The telephone went dead. Despite my protestations, David and his girlfriend insisted that I join them on the trip to Brighton, but I left my suitcase in the hall and came back to London that evening on the train.

'I'm so sorry, love,' said Daphne on Monday morning. 'My boyfriend got really annoyed, and it was all I could do to stop him from coming up to your flat. He's got a terrible temper on him.'

'Perhaps you shouldn't have told him,' I said.

'He wanted to take me dog racing on Saturday night, so I told him I had a work meeting. But he didn't believe me.'

'Well I won't ask you again, Daphne,' I said rather tetchily.

'No, best not,' she replied.

The senior partner sprang out of his office. 'Whitehall,

please can you get on with some work?' he said, and turning to Daphne, 'Nice weekend, Daphne?'

Having spent quite a lot of time in court during my first few weeks of articles, I decided that I had made a serious mistake in thinking that I wanted to be a solicitor. Solicitors seemed rather dull, dry, musty types, and I was finding the exams a real struggle. What I should be doing was studying for the Bar. A barrister in wig and gown, that was more my style. Nora concurred and bought me a wig in a very handsome tin box before I had even started as a student of the Middle Temple. At last I had found my niche.

Or so I thought. After I had eaten a few dinners in Middle Temple Hall and tried to get my head around Part I of the Bar examinations, I thought, is this really what I want or did I have my head turned by the costume department?

'You'll look so handsome in your wig and gown,' said Nora, but she didn't see me struggling with Part I of the Basic Tort Examination, and completely out of my depth.

'I'd cut and run,' said Jack. 'Your mother will be disappointed, but it's important that you do something you are going to enjoy. The wig and gown bit of a barrister's job is only a small part of it: it's the theatrical bit which presumably appealed to you.'

Jack's remarks reminded me of the father of an old Ampleforth friend of mine who was elected to the ceremonial office of deputy warden of something or other. He was a retired general in his late sixties, tall, with a fine curled moustache, a ramrod back and size twelve-and-a-half shoes. He found that while the range of pre-owned plumed hats, braided uniforms, jodhpurs and cloaks all fitted him, all the knee-length boots were far too small. He was authorized by the Warden's Office to go to the shoemakers Anello & Davide to have a brand-new pair made. He was attended by the manager of the shop, who said that, although they were primarily theatrical shoemakers, they would be able to make an excellent job of his ceremonial boots. When he returned for his final fitting the manager was on holiday, and he was looked after by a rather camp young assistant. Helping the general off with his hand-made Lobb brogues, he eased him into his handsome new boots. The general admired himself in the full-length mirror.

'Excellent,' he said to the assistant. 'A perfect fit. Wrap them up and I'll take them with me.'

'Right you are,' replied the assistant, 'they look a real treat.' And as he was boxing them up, he turned to the general and said: 'So what are you up to at the moment, love? Panto?'

3

Those Who Can't, Teach

There is a definite symmetry between looking after actors and looking after children. Having made a hash of my solicitor's articles and failed to get a grip on the Bar exams, I thought the soft option of a bit of prep school teaching might fill in some time while I decided what to do next. So I made my way to Messrs Gabbitas & Thring in Sackville Street, educational agents – if schoolmastering had been good enough for the likes of W. H. Auden, John Betjeman and Evelyn Waugh, then it might serve me equally well.

Mr Levy produced a number of vacancies typed neatly out on sheets of flimsy paper, the most promising of which he thought was one for an experienced geography teacher at Belmont School, run by a Mr Frank Sharples, MA. First-class games were also required. Unfortunately I offered neither of these.

'It doesn't do to be too modest,' said Mr Levy. 'It's wonderful what one can teach if one tries.'

I had, after all, scored more runs than the whole Ampleforth First XI put together, having been their scorer.

'What about the subsidiary biology?' I asked. 'I wouldn't know where to start. History and English are my subjects.'

'Don't worry,' Levy assured me, 'as long as you can keep them quiet, Sharples will be happy. Don't worry too much about teaching them anything at this stage. So do you want it?'

'What about an interview?' I asked.

'To be honest, Sharples is pretty desperate. He's just lost his senior master, who's gone off to be a monk; he's got two vacancies, and only a week before term starts. I'll fix it up for you on the telephone if you want it.'

A few days later I was sent a copy of my letter of engagement, which had several mistakes in it, including an Oxford degree which I certainly didn't have. It also mentioned the fact that I had been a 'member' of the First XI cricket team at Ampleforth, which seemed to be slightly stretching a point – but then stretching points seemed to be an integral part of the prep school world in the 1960s.

Belmont School, founded in 1880, was on Leith Hill, near Dorking in Surrey. The prospectus boasted of 'one hundred acres of woodland, all six hundred feet above sea level'. The school had 'a swimming bath, fruit and vegetable gardens, a bright and bracing environment, and provided the children exclusively with Grade (Tuberculin-Tested) "A" milk'. A fully qualified staff of 'graduate assistant masters' and one Froebel mistress were mentioned, along with an ex-army physical training instructor. There were eighty-eight boys, all boarders.

I took the precaution of removing the L-plates from my open-top Austin Nippy Sports before I swept up the drive. Although I had only a provisional driving licence, I thought L-plates weren't quite the right look at this stage. I'd taken a lot of trouble with my appearance: a tweed sports jacket, yellow foulard handkerchief and tie, set off by a rather natty brown felt hat bought in the Dunns sale. The final touch was a pipe, which I had enormous trouble in keeping alight, and which tasted disgusting. Good first impressions were important, although the removal of the L-plates proved to be a serious mistake.

The following morning, the headmaster asked me to go to Dorking Station to collect the luggage of the boys coming down from London. The boys themselves would return to the school in taxis accompanied by Mr Smith, the English master. I was taken to a lock-up garage where a rather battered-looking three-wheeler Reliant Robin van was parked. By now it was too late for me to reveal that I didn't have a driving licence. In any case, I thought, I'll only have the luggage on board.

I set off leaving plenty of time, but as I started going downhill, the Reliant developed a shudder and by the time I was into the forecourt of the station, it was stalling and backfiring. I drove up to the front of the station and found Mr Smith with a party of ten or so boys, plus luggage. Making their way towards me, however, were two uniformed policemen. As I introduced myself to Smith, with the boys giggling and crowding around their new teacher to get a closer look, I was tapped on the shoulder by one of the policemen.

'Are you in full control of this vehicle, sir?' said the constable.

'Absolutely . . . but it seems to be backfiring.'

'Quite apparently. Perhaps you're just not driving it properly. I would advise you to familiarize yourself with a vehicle before taking it on the public highway.'

'Yes, Officer. I'm sorry,' I spluttered, while trying to fit the luggage into the back of this ghastly unreliable Robin.

The boys clambered into the taxis, by now completely out of control. Mr Smith was almost totally blind and observed life through a selection of enormous magnifying glasses. Discipline was not his strong suit, and the boys knew it. He was also very tall; even if he'd been able to see properly, he would have been a long way from the action.

'You're from Belmont School aren't you, sir?' said the constable. 'I presume that if I were to ask you to produce your driving licence, you'd be in a position to do so.'

'Certainly,' I lied.

At this point, the taxis swept off leaving me with a policeman at either shoulder.

'Well, you'd better get off now sir, otherwise the boys won't have any luggage to unpack.'

They walked back and sat in their car. I started the van and halfway around the station forecourt the jerks started again. I glanced into the rear-view mirror and saw the officer taking out his notebook. Back up the hill and after a few more Vesuvian eruptions, the beastly thing came to a grinding halt. It then started rolling slowly backwards, so I pulled out a trunk and laid it across the wheels and set off for help.

'I gather you made a bloody fool of yourself at the station,' Mr Sharples bellowed down the telephone. (I was by now in a telephone box.) 'And there were police everywhere. What the hell's happened now?'

He told me that he had never had any trouble with the van before, and would send out the local garage.

The pick-up truck towed me up the drive of Belmont School and deposited me at the main entrance, in front of the boys, staff, matrons and what seemed like the entire population of Surrey. I had to dig deep to save what was left of my fragile dignity. The following morning I was to lose it completely.

'You're RC, aren't you, Whitehall?' said Mr Sharples over Sunday-morning breakfast. 'We have three RC boys here this term who have to go to Mass in Dorking at 10.30. I'd like you to take them. Your car's too small, and as you've buggered up the school van you'll have to use my car. I'll meet you outside my garage at ten.'

'Are you all right with automatics?' said Sharples, opening the garage doors the following morning.

'Absolutely,' I replied confidently.

There in front of me was a large, gleaming black Daimler limousine. As I slid into the soft leather-upholstered driver's seat, the boys – giggling, of course – followed me in.

'I'll see you out,' barked Sharples. 'Are you sure you're OK with automatics?'

'Of course,' I said assertively.

In fact I'd never been near an automatic car in my life and wasn't even sure what it was. I pressed the starter button, releasing a throbbing roar, and shoved the column-mounted stick into what I thought was an 'R' (but it turned out to be a '1'). I pressed my foot on the accelerator; the car shot forward and smashed into the back wall of the garage.

The veins on Mr Sharples's forehead, which resembled devil's horns, bubbled up as he gently reversed the car out of the garage, accompanied by the shattering sound of pieces of car falling on to concrete floor. The boys giggled again; the headmaster shook and I grovelled.

'I would suggest you get out of my sight before you demolish the whole bloody school,' barked Sharples, and I did.

' "*Get out of my sight before you demolish the whole bloody school*" '

Later, in the common room, once he'd calmed down, Sharples began to discuss the problems associated with my lack of a university degree.

'The prospectus says: "fully qualified staff"; I like to see a good sprinkling of MAs and BAs in the staff room. At present we're down to two amongst the lot of us; and to be honest Balantyne's doesn't really count as it's from a French university. I think I'll have to get you an FRGS,' he said.

'What's that, Headmaster?' I asked.

'Fellowship of the Royal Geographical Society.'

'But I'd never get one: I'm hopeless at geography; I failed it twice at O-level.'

'Don't worry about any of that, Whitehall,' he said. 'I'll get the forms.'

A week later, the headmaster sat over me while I completed a form, countersigned by him, stating that I was 'Head of Geography' – which I did subsequently become, due to the sudden departure of the geography master, but certainly wasn't then – and that I had travelled extensively and been on geological expeditions to Eastern China, the Nile Valley and Bhutan. In reality, the furthest abroad I had ever been was a week's holiday with my parents in Brittany. This didn't seem to trouble him in the slightest. He also invented a medal I'd received from an American college for research into Sanskrit, which seemed to me to have nothing to do with geography; but he was sure it would be helpful. A cheque for ten pounds was requested to accompany the application, on which he rather ungenerously suggested we went halves.

A few weeks later I received a letter from the Royal Geographical Society, informing me that I had been elected as a Fellow and enclosing a certificate confirming this election. Needless to say, Sharples suggested I had the certificate framed and hung in the staff room. On all future school notices, I was referred to as 'Michael Whitehall Esq., FRGS'.

The teaching staff, led by the eccentric Sharples, turned out to be a bizarre bunch of losers and misfits. Having shown me around the school – drawing my attention in particular to the canes, which were located in each classroom, in the common room and in all the staff bedrooms – I was introduced to my roommate, Brian Harris, a pale nervous young man of my own age with thick glasses and a mop of greasy black hair. I had assumed that I would have a bedroom of my own, but Sharples thought this arrangement would remind both Brian and me of our Varsity days. As neither of us had been to university, this seemed a strange bit of logic. Arriving outside the bedroom, Sharples was annoyed to discover that it was locked, with Harris inside.

'Why have you locked yourself in?' he bawled. 'You don't need to lock doors here.'

The door was opened by a shaking Harris who apologized profusely. Sharples escorted me in.

'Very odd behaviour indeed,' muttered the headmaster as he left Harris and me to get acquainted.

Brian was a sad individual. He screamed a lot during the night, and once told me he hated his parents. Poor chap, he was completely unable to control his class without the aid of a cane. On one occasion the boys managed to get hold of his cane and started beating him with it, causing such mayhem as to require the presence of an irate Sharples. A few days later Harris was dispatched on the milk train, leaving me unexpectedly with the geography portfolio, one of my specific Gabbitas & Thring exclusions. Well at least I had my fellowship on which to fall back.

Brigadier Adamson had retired from the Royal Tank Regiment at fifty-five, and had enrolled at a teachers' training college to get a Dip. Ed. with a view to teaching at a prep school. He didn't of course need a Dip. Ed., but he wanted to keep one step ahead of amateurs like me. His problem, however, was discipline.

As a brigadier in the army, he'd had a sergeant-major to get the parade in line; as a prep school master he was on his own. The noise from his classroom was deafening, and it was clear after a few weeks he wasn't going to make it. Unfortunately, the brigadier was another destined for the milk train, and I was now elevated to the position of Head of History, in addition to Head of Geography.

★　★　★

Marjorie Coxwell had no problems with discipline; the children were terrified of her. A tough, sixty-five-year-old lesbian, she had taught at Belmont for over thirty years and was well past her best. One afternoon, I opened the door of her classroom to discover that neither she nor her charges were there. She taught the junior form of seven- and eight-year-olds all subjects; and they stayed in the same room throughout the day, which I thought rather unfair.

'That's the way we've always done it here,' said Sharples.

So that was that. As I was about to close the door, a shaft of light picked out the face of a boy sitting behind his desk.

'Is there someone in there?' I asked.

'Yes, sir, we're all in here. It's Organ, sir,' replied the boy.

'Why are you sitting in the dark, Organ?'

'Miss Coxwell has got one of her migraines,' he whispered.

'So?'

'Well sir . . . when she has a migraine, we have to draw the curtains and sit in the dark in silence until she feels better.'

'And how long does that usually take?'

'Oh, sometimes a whole day, sir, but usually only a few hours.'

I closed the door and wondered what the parents of

these children would have made of it all, had they known.

And then there was Mr Woodley, the Head of Games. He had taught at Belmont before the war, and after a string of jobs at various second-rate prep schools had retired to the Channel Islands. With a short-notice vacancy in the games department, Sharples had invited him to come out of retirement and take over the First XV for the autumn term. Woodley was by now in his late seventies and although very tall (six foot five inches) was very stiff in the joints and had a pale, drooping head with a slight Parkinson's shake. He had the look of a man who had just stepped out of a coffin.

The first match of the term against Fernden was a disaster. Woodley arrived on the field in his full Selwyn College, Cambridge strip trying to look the business, but was clearly very breathless and found it increasingly difficult to keep up with the play. He was also wearing a hearing aid, which fell out of his ear every time he blew his whistle. Fernden were the strongest team on the circuit and after twenty-five minutes Belmont were losing 45–0. I was standing on the touchline with Mr Sharples.

'I've made a terrible mistake with Woodley,' he said. 'He was a wonderful games master here before the war, but I'd forgotten how long ago that was. He's clearly completely passed it – very embarrassing from a parental point of view.' I could feel another departmental head-ship coming my way.

After the match the headmaster offered me the position of Head of Games, another non-starter on my Gabbitas & Thring form. Mr Woodley was let go with a term's salary.

I too had problems keeping up with play when I refereed the following week's match. Having no kit, I wore a borrowed tracksuit and a pair of suede Chelsea boots. I could hardly keep my balance, and spent the match sliding across the pitch.

'You looked like a bloody ballet dancer out there,' said Sharples after the match. 'Get yourself some proper gear.'

I never really got to know Monsieur Balantyne, the French master, as he spoke virtually no English. This meant that the children learnt very little French. Bal-antyne's classes seemed to consist mainly of boys talking to each other in English while he shouted at them in French. He was no stranger to a generous Pernod before assembly; when prospective parents were shown around the school, Sharples had him confined to his room.

One evening I was sorting out the boys' boot room, following one of the headmaster's rants, when I sensed someone behind me.

'I could do with a bit of sorting out myself,' said Mrs Braine, the matron.

Rosemary Braine, thrice-married and thrice-divorced, was a busty woman in her forties with a shapely figure. I'd been warned that I was in her sights by Harris, who had had an unsuccessful fumble with her in the dispensary.

'She's very into young men,' he told me, 'but I don't think I was quite what she was looking for.'

Clearly I was.

As we flailed around among the Wellington boots, the door was flung open and there was Sharples.

'What the hell are you doing now, Whitehall? Get your hands off Matron.'

Fortunately, we were still fully dressed; although I think Mrs Braine might have removed her watch and thermometer, which had been pinned to her bosom.

I was finding my seventy-five guineas a term, payable termly in arrears, a bit of a tight squeeze, even though I was living at home in the holidays. Moreover, the social life at Belmont was becoming a little monotonous. Sometimes, it would be a glass of sherry in Monsieur Balantyne's room, which usually ran to a bottle and resulted in Balantyne's English becoming even more incoherent. As most of his conversations seemed to centre around the British having given up on the French far too early in the war and Churchill being almost single-handedly responsible for the German occupation in 1940, my drinking sessions with the Head of French became rare events.

The local pub was run by a bore called Bill Askey who claimed to be related to the comedian Arthur Askey. 'I was in show business before I went into the licence trade,' he said. 'Jack and Fifi Hylton were great mates – Fifi was real character.' Unfortunately Bill wasn't a real character: he was a phoney one and finally admitted that he hadn't actually met his cousin Arthur, but that their mothers were very close. A classic publican: he knew everything about everything, never listened and told me crude and unfunny jokes, roaring with laughter at the end of each one. 'You'll really like this one, Michael,' he'd say. And Michael didn't.

So it was time to move on. Frank Sharples didn't seem to be either surprised or disappointed at my decision.

'To be honest, I'd leave if I could,' he said over a large scotch in his study. 'But what else could I do? You've got youth on your side, so enjoy it and try and make some money. That's where I went wrong.'

One of the Belmont parents was in advertising. I wasn't entirely sure what that involved, but he was an engaging character, had a good-looking wife and an expensive car. So I thought I might take Sharples's advice and 'try and make some money'.

Scott Turner & Associates were certainly not in the top league of advertising agents, but having been turned down by J. Walter Thompson and Young & Rubicam, I thought that if I dropped a league (or two) I'd have more success. I did. Mr Scott Turner was looking for someone to train up as a copywriter, and my brief moment on the *Universe* at least got me through the door.

This was a time when advertising was king and people such as David Ogilvy were legends. I'd read somewhere that to be a successful copywriter you needed an obsessive curiosity about products and people, a habit of hard work and a sense of humour. Well, I could definitely tick the third box, but I wasn't sure about one and two.

Mr Scott Turner was a slick-looking man with a thin moustache and a penchant for sharp tweedy suits. He took me around the office (two floors in Dover Street) and left me in a room with a dishevelled-looking character called Raymond Massingham who was his senior copywriter. Raymond was clearly a disappointed man. A prematurely grey Oxford graduate, now in his late forties, he felt that advertising was beneath him; he had had aspirations to be a political journalist, had written a few unpublished novels and had just gone through a messy divorce.

'At least you've got youth on your side,' he said bitterly (where had I heard that before?), 'but copywriting is a dead-end job, and you never get any credit for it.'

Clearly his obsessive curiosity about products and people had long since waned.

'Have you done any writing?' he asked.

I told him that I had edited my school magazine and had spent a brief time on the *Universe* newspaper as their notional film critic and general dogsbody.

'I was a Catholic once,' he said. 'Lapsed now. Could never get to grips with transubstantiation – seemed too far-fetched. Take that away and there's not much left.'

'Is your wife Catholic?' I asked, more out of politeness than interest.

'Atheist. Thinks the whole thing is bollocks.'

Raymond hadn't exactly given me the most inspiring first morning in the advertising industry, and by the time I returned to his smoke-filled office after lunch I was feeling as depressed as he was.

'We're doing some point-of-sale cards for a firm in Leeds that makes shoetrees. Also some local newspaper ads. All black-and-white. Do you want to have a stab at some copy? I've run out of ideas.'

Now although I knew Scott Turner & Associates weren't in the front rank of agencies, I assumed they would still have some pretty classy clients to pay their rent in Dover Street. If not Cadbury's, then at least Fry's. I hadn't asked Scott Turner who his clients were at my original meeting as I'd thought he would raise the subject. He didn't.

'I'm going out for half an hour. See what you can come up with. They'll want to see some stuff tomorrow.'

I tried to summon up some curiosity about shoetrees and jotted down a few ideas. The company was called Shoeshape and in addition to trees they made shoeboxes, shoebrushes and shoehorns. Fortunately we were only asked to get behind their trees. 'GIVE YOUR SHOES A

TREAT WITH SHOESHAPE TREES'. Perhaps not quite as eye-catching as 'GUINNESS IS GOOD FOR YOU' or 'YOU CAN BE SURE OF SHELL', but not a bad start.

'I KEEP MY SHOES IN SHAPE WITH SHOESHAPE SHOETREES – THE QUALITY TREES', I wrote out in my best handwriting. Mmm. I was beginning to get the feel for this; I couldn't wait for Raymond to return from wherever he'd gone and discuss my ideas with him. When he did return, an hour or so later, he looked very bleary and had clearly been in the pub next door to the office.

'I got a high 2.1 in history at Cambridge University, and now I'm writing copy for a load of fucking shoetree makers in Leeds.'

'Well actually, I've come up with a couple of ideas. Presumably there is going to be a picture of the shoetrees on the card?'

'Presumably,' he slurred.

'And somebody holding them?' I asked.

'Possibly,' he yawned, 'if they can afford a model,' and slumped into an ash-covered armchair.

'Well, how about a male model in a naval uniform, holding up trees and saying: "I keep my shoes shipshape with Shoeshape Shoetrees." What do you think?' I asked eagerly.

He'd fallen asleep.

The following morning he greeted me with: 'We're pitching for the Munchies account – come up with some copy.'

I'd never heard of Munchies, an obscure chocolate product made in the North somewhere.

'Only media, they can't afford anything else.'

So Raymond and I got to work, and together came up with the unforgettable line:

'HERE COME NEW CRUNCHIER MUNCHIES'.

Even Raymond was pleased.

'It's not a new product,' said the account executive at a meeting that afternoon.

'And they aren't any crunchier than they were before,' said the brand manager.

'So what the fuck are we being hired for?' snapped Raymond. 'To tell the truth, is Guinness *actually* good for you?'

Raymond was clearly at the end of his tether, and I sensed a resignation in the air. Back in his office Raymond told me that he was looking around for another job, away from advertising. 'I've got a good degree for Christ's sake. What *am* I doing here?'

A few weeks later he told me that he was leaving at the end of the month.

'I've decided to teach for a bit while I make up my mind,' he said. 'I've been to an educational agency called Gabbitas & Thring, and they say that with my degree I could have the pick of prep schools. Didn't you do some teaching?'

'Yes, I did actually. At a school called Belmont.'

'I've got a feeling that's one of the schools on my list.'

★ ★ ★

Raymond's replacement was not me, as I'd hoped, but a rather pushy and smug Old Etonian, whose father was managing director of one of Scott Turner's main clients. He took an instant dislike to me, and as the feeling was mutual, it seemed time for me to move on too. But I couldn't face going back to teaching. Fortunately, I spotted an advertisement in the *Daily Telegraph* for an organizing secretary for something called the Keystone Cops. 'KEYSTONE COPS: THE NATIONAL ASSOCIATION OF BOYS' CLUBS SEEKS ORGANIZING SECRETARY FOR FUNDRAISING COMMITTEE. PREVIOUS EXPERIENCE OF FUNDRAISING ESSENTIAL. GRADUATE PREFERRED.' Well, I hadn't had any experience of fundraising, apart from trying to keep my own finances afloat with the help of my parents, and it did say graduate *preferred*, not essential. I did at least have my FRGS, thanks to Frank Sharples. Interviews were being held for short-listed candidates at the Dorchester Hotel in a month's time. I sent my application in with muted enthusiasm.

I had a preliminary meeting with the secretary of the NABC. at their offices in Bedford Square, where I also met the chairman, who happened to be passing through. Viscount Althorp meant nothing to me at the time. The meeting went well, although my lack of experience seemed to be a worry. A few days later I received a letter summoning me to the Dorchester Hotel the following week to meet members of the Keystone Cops, for whom I would be working. They were a group of rich

Nora joins the Whitehall family

ack in his Old Cranleighan tie

Uncle Peter – the dashing major

My mother never let me forget she had always wanted a girl

In the shadow of Margate Pier

Our male dog, Candy, was traumatized by having a bitch's name

Whitehall and Rothwell (centre front) in cross-country mode

At the Ampleforth Exhibition Weekend with cousin Jennifer

Pushing the boat out at the Café de Paris with Eileen

Nora in her gardening clothes

Belmont School: 'A bright and bracing environment'

The reluctant Head of Games

Modelling for Mr Fish (photo by Lichfield)

The nearest Tiny Tim ever got to a
Playboy bunny

One more for the road . . .

Julian resisting a hug from Kenneth More

With Julian, Amanda and Stephen, 'putting the smile back into showbusiness' at 60 St James's Street

businessmen and show-business personalities who raised money for boys' clubs through fundraising events. It was the secretary's job to organize these events.

I was the third of three candidates awaiting a grilling. The first was a red-faced, overweight and rather sweaty man in his forties who kept up a running commentary as the various members of the committee arrived for the meeting.

'Evelyn de Rothschild, the banker,' he whispered to me, as a tall elegant middle-aged man strolled past. 'Worth a few bob,' he added.

'Good morning,' said the next arrival.

'Good morning,' said the sweaty man with a particularly obsequious leer, and then to me behind his hand, 'Dickie Attenborough, the actor, a lovely man.'

Did he know Dickie, as he referred to him? I thought probably not. And then a huddle of banker types appeared, gossiping to each other, together with a few faces I recognized – Colin Ingleby-Mackenzie, Algy Cluff, Victor Lownes, Frankie Vaughan and, king of the wrestling world, Jarvis Astaire.

'Hello, Brian,' said a man behind them to the third member of our party, who had hitherto remained silent, 'how's tricks?'

'Fine, thanks, Roy. And yourself?' It was Roy Castle, the multi-talented comedian, singer and trumpeter. He then dashed into the ballroom, closing the doors behind him.

'You know Roy, then?' said Mr Sweaty to Brian.

'Yes, great bloke. He did a lot of work for the NSPCC when I was with them.'

Damn, I thought, Brian's had experience; they're bound to go for him or Mr Sweaty, who seems to know everyone. At which point, the doors reopened.

'Brian, do come in,' said a trendy-looking man with long hair and a strong resemblance to the fashion photographer, Patrick Lichfield. So he knew Brian too. It looked like a shoo-in to me. Brian was in there for ages; Mr Sweaty, who was even more sweaty when he came out, for less than five minutes.

'They want you to go in, although I think they've made their minds up already.' He glared at Brian, who was sitting on the sofa, looking very pleased with himself and flicking through *Man About Town*.

'Now, Mr Whitehall,' said Mr Attenborough, 'tell us about yourself.'

A dozen pairs of eyes bored into me. My throat was dry and I was beginning to shake slightly. I wish I'd read that book *Interview Technique*, which Nora had bought me the previous day.

'Well,' I said tentatively, 'where shall I start?'

'At the beginning?' said Colin Ingleby-Mackenzie and laughed, putting me instantly at ease. I joined in and then, as if possessed of some alien spirit, I launched into an anecdotal history of my life, peppered with jokes and the occasional funny voice. When I returned to the anteroom, Brian said bitterly, 'Well, you certainly kept them amused.'

The doors reopened.

'Thank you so much for coming in,' said Attenborough. 'We'll be in touch.'

Having taken up residence at 17 Bedford Square, I set about helping to organize various fundraising events around the country. These included everything from fashion shows and film premières to cricket, golf and wrestling matches, not to mention a series of pop concerts at the Albert Hall. The concerts were the most successful events, starting with the Byrds and culminating in the extraordinary phenomenon that was Tiny Tim. Our first concert had done very well, and when Tiny Tim's manager telephoned to ask if we would like to have Tiny for our next concert, I immediately said yes.

Tiny Tim had been singing for twenty years before he was noticed at Hubert's Flea Circus in New York. With shoulder-length hair and Elizabeth Arden make-up, he sang in a high falsetto voice and strummed a ukulele. 'Tiptoe Through the Tulips' was his big hit.

I had to escort Tiny to various press and PR interviews, including a photo-shoot with the Earl of Snowdon at *The Sunday Times*. Tiny became very excited as we took the lift up to the penthouse.

'Do I call him "Your Majesty"?' he asked. 'Oh, what a great honour to be photographed by royalty.'

' ''Do I call him Your Majesty'' '

Later he was photographed by Patrick Lichfield.

'He's an earl as well, isn't he, Mr Whitehall?' said Tiny on our way to Lichfield's studio in Aubrey Walk. 'Is he royalty too?'

Obviously nothing like this had ever happened to him at Hubert's Flea Circus.

Before Tiny arrived in London, I was sent a list of his various cosmetic and dietary requirements, with his personal comments scribbled in.

AIDA GREY'S PEACH MILK CLEANSING CREAM

PORE CLEANSER

MINT MILK

ROOT OF LIFE NIGHT CREAM

SKIN LOTION

MAKE-UP

You'll see a change right away when your face says hello to Aida Grey. T. T.

PAPAYA TOOTH POWDER

POLLY BERGEN'S OIL OF TURTLE SOAP

ELIZABETH ARDEN'S BLUE GRASS HAND LOTION

In any garden, it's Elizabeth Arden

JOHNSON'S BABY LOTION

PRETTY FEET

WHISPER MOUTH SPRAY

A spray a day keeps the bad breath away. T. T.

And on the dietary front . . .

SUNFLOWER SEEDS

ORGANIC PUMPKIN SEEDS

WHEAT GERM

PEAK'S PURE RAW UNFILTERED TUPELO HONEY

CARNATION MALTED MILK

VANILLA GREAT SHAKES *(must be made in a Great Shakes shaker). T.T.*

A VERY OCCASIONAL LETTUCE AND TOMATO SANDWICH ON WHOLE WHEAT. *T.T.*

The concert was a great success: Tiny was backed by a thirty-piece orchestra, conducted by Richard Perry, plus Joe Cocker, Peter Sarstedt and the Bonzo Dog Doo Dah Band, who gave Tiny a run for his money in terms of eccentricity.

For a moment it looked as though Elvis Presley might make his first visit to England and top the bill at our next Albert Hall concert. His manager, Colonel Tom Parker, was very warm on the telephone, but when we got into the fine detail, it was clearly going to be a non-starter. Elvis would appear for free; the cost of transporting and accommodating both his entourage and him would have bankrupted us.

Around this time, I received a letter from two young composers asking for a meeting to discuss their participation in our next concert. When they arrived at Bedford Square, they left their bicycles in the hall and handed me a recording of a musical, which thus far had been performed only by the students of St Paul's School. Could it be presented at the Albert Hall by the Keystone Cops? This sounded like a no-hoper. I had been trying to get Elvis and even had a contact working on the Beatles. A group of singing schoolchildren really wasn't what we were looking for. I told them it was bit of a long shot, though I'd be delighted to listen to the recording. Although much impressed by it, I didn't think it really fitted the bill as far as we were concerned. I called them a few days later and wished them well with their quest. Needless to say, Tim Rice and Andrew Lloyd Webber found a home for *Joseph and His Amazing Technicolor Dreamcoat* without my help.

As secretary of the Keystone Cops I was responsible for relatively large quantities of cash taken at our fundraisers. The money collected at these events, which usually finished in the small hours of the morning, would be stuffed into a leather holdall, which I would then have to take home overnight. The following morning I would hand over the proceeds to the accounts department.

On one occasion, after a boxing event at the Café Royal, I was brushing my teeth and ruminating on a successful evening's fundraising, when I broke out in a cold sweat. I knew I had taken the holdall into the cab with me, but had I taken it out when I got back to Barnes? I raced out of the bathroom, only to find the hallway empty – no bag. I couldn't be sure exactly how much money was in the bag, but certainly well over

£1,000. It was no use trying to sleep, so I telephoned the lost property office of the Licensed Taxi Drivers' Association. As it was now 3 a.m., I wasn't surprised to discover that they shut at 6 p.m. and reopened at 8 a.m. But would anyone hand in a bag of cash? No way. I spent what was left of the night praying.

'Lost property,' said the stern voice at the end of the line.

I explained the situation.

'I'll look.'

I hung on for several minutes, my heart in my mouth.

'Did you say a black leather bag?' said the voice.

'Y-yes, have you got it?' I said hopefully.

'We do, but you'll have to come in and identify it.'

'Right . . .' I hesitated. 'Is there anything in it?' I added as casually as I could.

' . . . no.'

'Nothing at all?' Surely a few fivers at the bottom of the bag, I thought?

'Just hang on a minute, I need to check something with a colleague.' The voice was becoming even sterner.

'Good morning,' said a friendly voice. 'I'm just going off duty, but I did take a bag in earlier from one of our drivers.'

'Right.'

'Do you live in Lillian Road, Barnes?'

'Yes, I do.'

'Was there anything in the bag when you left it in the cab?'

'Well, yes, there was.'

'May I ask what?'

'Quite a lot of cash, actually.'

'Do you know how much?'

'Not really; I didn't have time to count it.'

'Are you a burglar?'

'What?'

'I said, are you a burglar?'

He had a point: people don't usually go around with bags full of cash.

'No, of course not,' I said angrily. I was beginning to get tetchy (I hadn't slept for twenty-four hours).

'Only joking, sir.'

'The bag contained the proceeds from a fundraising event at the Café Royal last night.'

'Then you'll be pleased to hear that you've raised £1,755, sir. Congratulations.'

Phew. I rushed off to the Angel.

'Luckily for you, you were the driver's last fare of the night,' said the office manager. 'If he'd taken any fares after you, they would certainly have nicked it. But our drivers are very honest.'

Lying on his desk was a large, translucent plastic envelope, in which the money was neatly sorted.

'So, that's £1,755 in all, sir, less our 15 per cent for the Benevolent Fund. That comes to £1,493.'

By the time I arrived at the office, I'd developed the shakes. How could I have been so stupid and careless, and yet so unbelievably lucky? Perhaps those Hail Marys had done the trick.

'Good morning, Michael,' said the General Secretary, as I passed him in the hall. 'I gather last night was a great success. I've just been speaking to David Westmorland, who wants you to ring him.'

I went straight to accounts and handed over the money.

'I see you've counted it all,' said the accounts clerk. 'Very efficient.'

'Well, I like to do things properly. There's £1,493 there, but check it just in case.'

'The Earl of Westmorland on the phone for you,' said the switchboard girl.

'How did we do, Michael?'

'Ticket sales et cetera came to over £2,000 and cash £1,493.'

'Well done, excellent work. See you at the meeting on Wednesday.'

The meeting at the Dorchester was to discuss Keystone's future. After ten years of fundraising, several of the members felt that it was time to call it a day. More importantly, no one felt like recruiting new fundraisers. I had also decided it was time for me to move on, again. Once the meeting was over, I was approached by Robin Fox, one of the members who had originally interviewed me for the job. If I didn't have any firm plans for the future, would I be interested in meeting his business partner, Laurie Evans, with a view to joining their actors' agency? Well, that might fill in a few months, I thought.

4

The Agent Comes of Age

As I arrived in Hanover Street for my first day at London International, I bumped into my new boss, Laurie Evans, getting out of his chauffeur-driven Rolls-Royce. Laurie was a tall, bespectacled, balding man of sixty, who looked more like a family solicitor than an actors' agent. A creature of habit, he was always soberly dressed in well-tailored grey suits and plain ties, with not a hint of the flamboyance normally associated with the theatrical world.

'I made a fatal mistake when Tony joined me,' he muttered. 'I didn't close the partition on day one, and by day two it was too late. It's not just that he never stops talking, but it's all such boring stuff: weather, traffic jams, short cuts, all that sort of thing. You know what I mean?'

Having never had a chauffeur, I didn't really but nodded politely in agreement. I would certainly have been far too embarrassed to close the glass partition on my chauffeur; I found it difficult enough with cab drivers. Being in the back of cabs with well-known faces always brings out the worst in cab drivers. There is a lot of winking, I-know-you looks, and so-what-are-you-up-to-then-behaving-yourself? jokes.

As we went up in the lift to the top floor, Laurie explained that I would be working for him, his partner Robin Fox, as well as for a new arrival from the States, Otis S. Blodget.

'Blodget's a bit of an acquired taste, but you know Robin of course.'

I knew Robin, father of the Fox brothers, Edward, James and Robert, through the Keystone Cops. Robin was a contemporary of Laurie's. Tall and dashing with a lethargic manner that belied a very keen business mind, he called his clients 'ducky', something I would never have dared to do.

I had been taken to Scott's by Laurie and Robin for Laurie to give me the once-over. After lunch I had a long chat with Tony through the open partition, while Laurie and Robin talked business to Lew Grade on the pavement outside the restaurant.

'I'm going to avoid Berkeley Square when I take you back to the office,' he said. 'There's a road works on the Piccadilly side near Hay Hill; the traffic there this morning was a nightmare. It took us twenty minutes to get from Mr Evans's flat to the office. Normally it's a ten-minute run. Still, it gave us a chance to have a chat. I've been with Mr Evans for ever, but I still don't feel that I really know him.'

Laurie and Robin offered me the job in the back of the car, as Tony was trying to avoid a build-up of traffic in Old Bond Street, and I started work a month or so later.

Laurie's assistant, Frances, gave me a tour of the offices laid out over three floors of a sleek modern building on the corner of Hanover Street and Hanover Square. I was introduced to the other agents and then ushered into Otis S. Blodget's room. Mr Blodget's secretary seemed to be clearing up some papers under his desk, and both looked startled at our sudden appearance.

'Mr Blodget, this is Michael Whitehall, your new assistant,' Frances beamed.

Blodget stood up and strode around his large desk to shake my hand. I noticed that his fly buttons were undone.

'Dick Blodget, but call me Dick. Come on in and take a seat,' he boomed.

Blodget's secretary Diana, a nervous girl with unruly hair, scooped up an armful of letters and disappeared. Blodget explained that he had recently arrived from New York. The company had been taken over by an American agency, and he was the advance guard. Laurie and Robin still ran the show, but he was there to keep a watching brief. We were both new boys, he said, giving me a wink. I hoped he didn't think I was going to be the company sneak. I also hoped that he'd realize his flies were undone. I didn't think I knew him well enough to make allusions to 'open stable-doors' and 'flying low'.

'I've got a lunch meeting with Deke Hayward at the Ivy. He's head of production at AIP. Why don't you come along?'

'How are the testicles, Deke?' asked Dick over the potted shrimps. Mr Hayward went into all the gory details: pain in the left one, swelling in the right one, and then two days in the London Clinic while they drained the fluid from both. I sat in silence. Had I got it wrong yet again? Did I really want to be an actors' agent? Was Nora right? Surely a barrister wouldn't have had to sit through *this*? Dick and Deke then got down to business. A film Deke was making needed a beautiful girl to play the lead – preferably blonde, big tits, long legs, ideally English (but could be dubbed). Had we got anyone?

'Michael?' asked Dick.

I hadn't even seen the client list, and certainly not the big-titted-blonde section.

'I'll come back to you, Deke,' I said.

'What about Ingrid Pitt?' said Dick. 'You'd get distribution with Ingrid, Deke. Michael, fix it for Deke to meet Ingrid.'

'Right,' I stammered.

During lunch at Les Ambassadeurs, Ingrid, whom I had only just met, accidentally touched my knee under the table and gave me a broad smile.

'I want to be Michael's client,' she said to Dick.

'Of course Ingrid, a very good idea.'

Deke was much taken by Ingrid, and the fact that she was a thirty-two-year-old Pole didn't seem to worry him, even though the part of Mary McPhail was written as a seventeen-year-old Scottish peasant girl.

Dick then told us one of Laurie's stories about John Gielgud, who was invited for the weekend to an Elizabethan manor house near Stroud, owned by friends of a friend. Although not overly keen on staying in other people's houses, he was assured that he would be enchanted not only by his hosts but also by their beautiful house. He was not disappointed.

Staying in the Chinese Room, a grand boudoir facing the garden with antique silk curtains and rare hand-coloured Chinese wallpaper, his light was out before midnight. A few hours later, he awoke to discover that he was in urgent need of the lavatory. The room was pitch dark, and in trying to reach for the bedside lamp he knocked something over on the table. Feeling his way to the door he flicked on the light switch and was about to open the bedroom door when he realized that his hands were covered in black ink. He looked over to the table by the bed and saw that he had knocked over an inkwell. The full horror of what had happened hit him; across the priceless antique Chinese wallpaper was a trail from the bed to the door of inky handprints. Too devastated even to attempt any kind of explanation for the ghastliness of this grisly scene, he quickly packed his bags, crept down the stairs, and drove home.

Some years later, he was invited to tea at a nearby house. He arrived early just as the house party were heading off for a post-lunch walk. To his horror, in the middle of the group, putting on her Wellingtons, was the lady of the house, the woman with the Chinese wall-paper. They both pretended they hadn't met before, and John opted to wait in the drawing room until they returned from their walk. Relaxing in a comfortable armchair in front of a blazing fire he nodded off. When he awoke, he heard a strange muffled whine coming from the seat of his chair. He got up to put a log on the fire, and as he was about to sit down again he noticed a small white furry ball protruding from underneath one of the heavy damask cushions. He lifted the cushion to reveal his hostess's white Chihuahua, which had clearly been suffocated under John's weight. He picked the dog up, shook it and then put it down on the floor. It was clearly dead. John grabbed his hat and coat and headed for the car. The story seemed to have no relevance to our meeting, and probably wasn't even true, but it did take the pressure off me for a bit.

'Let's have supper one evening *soon*,' Ingrid purred, as I headed back to the office.

I later explained to Laurie that having just got married (my first marriage, not the one in Withyham), I wasn't really looking for anything extra-marital just at the moment.

'It's important for the film,' said Laurie. 'Ingrid is having an affair with a big cheese at the Rank Organization. If she does the film, it will get distribution. We also represent the producer, director and writer as well as Ingrid, so it's important she's kept sweet.'

'But what if the man at Rank finds out? He won't be pleased.'

'It's not a physical thing with him; for God's sake, he's in his seventies. He just likes having her around, and I'm sure he'll appreciate the help,' said Laurie.

This really didn't tally with Laurie's earlier advice: 'Fuck William Morris's clients by all means, but don't fuck ours.'

Ingrid and I had supper, and back at her flat I tried, with great difficulty, to parry her advances, while not causing offence. My non-existent client list needed at least one name on it. But how far was I willing to go to achieve it? I tried to get the conversation round to Hitler's seizure of Danzig and the Polish Corridor in 1939. Ingrid would have none of it: the only corridor she was interested in was the one leading to the bedroom.

'I think we need to get our relationship on a business footing before we move on to the personal area,' I said. 'It's not going to be easy for me, Ingrid, but I'm sure it's the right way forward.'

★   ★   ★

One of my early learning curves was 'looking after' ladies of a certain age – Dorothy Lamour, Dawn Addams, Jill Bennett, Honor Blackman, Glynis Johns, Rachel Roberts, Coral Browne, Adrienne Corrie and Shelley Winters. A formidable bunch.

'Extend all courtesies,' insisted Miss Lamour's LA agent. 'She's a great lady and absolutely no trouble.'

The technical term for keeping an eye on an overseas client while they're in London is 'servicing'. And Miss Lamour certainly needed servicing on a regular basis.

As I waited to meet her at Heathrow, I was expecting Bob Hope and Bing Crosby's romantic interest in *The Road to Rio*. The apparition struggling with her suitcase would have been more comfortable on a zimmer frame than in a sarong. She was now in her mid-sixties, though time hadn't been kind to her and she looked ten years older. On our way to the hotel, she explained that her visit was a social one; she had some distant relatives living in Wales who were coming to London to see her, but she would also like some meetings with casting directors and producers while she was in town. She became rather curt with me when I broached the question of her 'playing age'.

'I play forty,' she told me very firmly. I remember hearing a snigger from the elderly cab driver.

'Really enjoyed you in *The Jungle Princess*, Dorothy,' he said, as we arrived at the Dorchester. It was a film of which I'd never heard. 'Nineteen thirty-six you made that. My parents took me to see it at the Empire in Leicester Square.'

Miss Lamour looked a little flustered as I was left wondering, 'If she plays forty now and *The Jungle Princess* was in 1936 – forty years ago – how old does that make her?' But I thought it might be best to leave the subject alone until we got to know one another better.

'Who?' said Maud Spector, doyenne of casting directors. 'Surely she's not still at it?'

'Well, she's in London for meetings and I thought you might like to see her.'

'I'll get back to you,' said Maud, and didn't.

In fact the only meeting I managed to get her was with a TV producer who was planning a remake of *Great Expectations* and thought she'd make a terrific Miss Havisham.

Miss Lamour was not amused; and returned to the States without even saying goodbye. Well at least I wasn't expected to service her, which was more than could be said about Dawn Addams. Now, she definitely had servicing on her mind.

'Dick tells me you've always been an admirer of mine,' she said as we left the office on our way to lunch. 'How *very* flattering.'

Flattering perhaps, but really unfair, as Dick knew. He told me that Miss Addams had recently come through a very messy and public divorce (from an Italian prince), and was in a highly charged emotional state. I went rather further than I had planned to with Miss Addams, but I felt it was all part of my learning curve and, to an extent, Dick set me up for it.

'Get yourself some clients,' said Laurie one Monday morning after a fraught drive from his house in Sussex with Tony, who had taken a detour around Kingsfold due to resurfacing on the A24. 'Servicing other people's clients won't get you anywhere.'

'We should have gone A264,' said Tony helpfully once they were on the A23.

Laurie had a smart flat just behind Berkeley Square where he stayed during the week and a beautifully lacustrine, manicured estate on the edge of Horsham in West Sussex for weekends. His clients, Laurence Olivier, John Gielgud, Ralph Richardson, John Mills, Kenneth More, Albert Finney and Rex Harrison, were regular guests. He was primarily an actors' agent. 'Actresses are very time-consuming,' he once warned me, although he did find time to represent the occasional Dame. The agent Freddie Joachim took this a step further and wouldn't look after actresses or married couples at all. 'Too difficult,' he said.

One of my early duties was to extract Laurie's clients from commitments they never had any intention of fulfilling, usually arranged at social functions and often involving personal friends. It was my job to ensure that no blame was ever attached to the actor; these broken promises were always the result of a misunderstanding or confusion over dates. Not true, of course. Actors tell people what they want to hear, which is usually 'yes'; though the agent can always be blamed further down the line when the 'yes' turns to 'no'.

Seasons at obscure reps, plays written by unknown writers, unfinanceable films and appearances at book festivals and poetry readings – this was my world. I took care of the radio interviews while Laurie looked after the Hollywood movies.

'But Sir Laurence said he'd definitely be there,' said the organizer of the Aberystwyth Arts Festival. 'I met him outside the Old Vic last night; I suppose you've talked him out of it.'

'Albert Finney was born in Salford, you know,' said the President of the West Manchester Christian Union. 'He told me he'd consider it an honour to open our new reading room next month. What's made him change his mind? You no doubt.' And so on.

But looking after other people's clients was not the route to the top, as Laurie kept reminding me – although he probably hadn't envisaged that my first big client would come off his own list. Kenneth More was a legend, but by the mid-1970s, a slightly fading one, and Laurie wasn't returning his telephone calls with the alacrity that he'd come to expect. His move from boss to assistant wasn't an easy one, but it did at least absolve Laurie from the responsibility of suggesting Kenny for jobs. Laurie didn't like suggesting clients for jobs.

'Producers then think you owe them a favour. Let them ring you,' he said.

And it did show that I was listening. Laurie had talked to me a lot about *unsettling* other people's clients, with a view to 'poaching' them. For example, at a glittering first-night party in the West End, I'd ask an actor about his agent.

'Is she OK?'

'Yes, fine. Why?'

'Only that – no forget it.'

'No, please, what do you mean, "OK"?'

'Well it's just that I'd heard, I'm sure wrongly, that she'd started drinking again.'

'What do you mean *again*? I didn't know she drank?'

'Look, forget it. I should never have mentioned it, not after all that earlier trouble.'

'What earlier trouble?' And so forth.

And later.

'Are you up for the new Lean movie?'

'What movie?'

'I'm sure your agent's suggested you for it. You'd be perfect for the young lead. All my clients have already met for it.'

'I'll get on to my agent in the morning.'

'I certainly would, or why not call tonight?'

'I don't have her home number.'

'What! I don't believe it. Who are you with again?'

And then, the more direct approach.

'I gather your agent's leaking clients.'

'Really?'

'Yes, I hear Johnny has gone.'

'No?'

'I think so, and Vanessa.'

'God, I'd no idea. Who else?'

'I honestly can't remember and I may be completely wrong, but I hear there's been a pretty major rush for the exit. A shame, because I really like . . .'

And, if you're lucky enough to meet the actor on a film set.

'Well at least they're paying well.'

'I'm not being well paid.'

'Really? Maybe I was just lucky, but I got a great deal for Nigel. Obviously it took time, but I got there in the end.'

'My agent said he'd had to take what they offered. Take it or leave it they said.'

'That does surprise me. Who are you with again?'

Laurie told me that, in the old days, good agents in London were very rich: they all had villas in the South of France and would go away in August. He discovered that their clients, who were in the theatre or films, couldn't get away in August and were very easy game. He would take them out to lunch and say: 'It must simply be awful not having your agent around, is there any way I can help?'

So I followed my mentor's example and took on Kenneth More and Harry Andrews, another of Laurie's clients in need of attention. Shortly after Harry moved over to me, he invited me to dinner at his house in East Sussex, which he shared with his actor friend, Basil Hoskins. I was nervous about staying the night at their strictly 'men only' cottage, though I was delighted to discover Harry's lady housekeeper in residence. Harry's housekeeper had been in love with him for years, and although the bedroom department was strictly reserved for Basil, she always escorted Harry to film premières, awards ceremonies, and even appeared with him on 'This is Your Life'. It was clear over dinner that neither of them was wildly enthusiastic about my being there. I was Harry's new agent, relatively young – well certainly twenty years younger than they were – and heterosexual, a bonus in my favour as far as Harry was concerned. To have been able to seduce a young straight man who was also his agent – well, cats and cream weren't in it. Nevertheless, it was not to be, despite a huge amount of attention going into the sleeping arrangements. I was particularly pleased that I had packed some thick winceyette pyjamas and a woollen dressing gown.

Having specifically asked Harry not to wake me in the morning with a cup of tea, as I had brought my alarm clock, he burst into my bedroom at nine o'clock with a huge tray of breakfast: bacon and eggs, toast, fruit juice and assorted pots of marmalade and honey. As I struggled to sit up in bed and do up my pyjamas at the same time, I caught Harry's hand with my elbow. He gave me a leering smile.

'Good morning Manager,' he cooed. 'A little surprise for you.' At which point, he lost his footing and tumbled on to the bed. The tray flew out of his hands, and I was covered with tea, juice, toast and pieces of bacon, which Harry attempted to retrieve from under the sheets. I leapt out of bed, grabbed my dressing gown and started pulling the soaking sheets off the mattress; at which point Basil appeared at the bedroom door.

'So what are you two up to?' he asked. 'Breakfast in bed, eh?'

And so the client list continued to grow, with a few more cast-offs and hand-me-downs – Patrick Macnee, Anton Diffring (the Nazi officer specialist), Honor Blackman, Mark Burns – and some new clients of my own, such as Dinsdale Landen. Dinsdale was riding high in West End plays, such as *The Philanthropist*, *Alphabetical Order*, *London Assurance* and *Plunder* and television series in between. But like most actors, Dinsdale hated being out of work and he had a gap in his schedule that he was anxious to fill.

'I'd really like you to meet Cameron Mackintosh,' said Dinsdale. 'He's young, enthusiastic and really nice, and wants me to do a tour for him.'

'But is he any good?' I asked. 'I've never heard of him. Do you really need to go out on some random tour for an unknown producer?'

'Well, at least meet him,' said Dinsdale.

'Does he have any money? Will we get paid?' I asked.

Dinsdale persevered, and I finally made an appearance at Dinsdale's house in Putney. Sitting on the banquette in his sitting room was Cameron. He leapt up. Cameron was indeed very young, very enthusiastic and very nice; but in my newly acquired judgement, he had the look of a loser about him. We had a jolly lunch talking almost exclusively about Dinsdale's career, and Cameron left us on the warmest of terms.

'I'll call you tomorrow, Cameron,' said Dinsdale encouragingly.

Dinsdale was eager to know what I thought of his new friend.

'He's really nice, isn't he?' he said. 'And very enthusiastic about me.'

'And very young,' I said. 'Do you think he knows what he's doing? And do you really want to do a fifteen-week tour of *Dandy Dick*?'

'No, not really, unless you think . . .' said Dinsdale.

'Do you want to ring him, or shall I?' I asked.

'Maybe it would be better if you did,' he replied. 'I'll write to him later.'

As we walked to my car, I told Dinsdale that I thought that Cameron was far too star-struck. He looked like someone who'd come a cropper very easily and, of course, if the whole thing went wrong, it would be entirely my fault. Dinsdale concurred. He knew I was right. We'd pass on *Dandy Dick*.

I read recently that Cameron is now worth over £500 million, and has houses in London and New York, as well as a thirteen-thousand-acre estate in the Scottish highlands, a farm in Somerset and a vineyard in Provence. I've got a house in Putney with a large mortgage and a matching overdraft. The look of a loser indeed.

A few days later I was walking across Putney Common with Dinsdale when we were approached by an attractive middle-aged woman.

'I know you, don't I?' she said to Dinsdale; the usual form of address when meeting an actor whose face you recognize.

'You're off that TV show aren't you? What's it called? You're Linstall, aren't you?'

Dinsdale gave the lady a charming smile. 'Dinsdale Landen, actually.'

'That's it, Dinstall. Ooooh, you're one of my favourites. I love that series you're in.'

'Oh, "Pig in the Middle", you mean,' said Dinsdale helpfully.

'No, the other one.'

Dinsdale couldn't remember another one.

'May I introduce my manager, Michael Whitehall?' said Dinsdale.

I was not used to being introduced to people as their manager. Kenneth More told me that his first agent always asked him to refer to him as his manager, especially when they were abroad. 'Agent always sounds common,' he told Kenny, 'particularly on the continent.' Dinsdale evidently thought it sounded a bit common in Putney too.

'Oh, I'm such a fan,' oozed the lady on the common. 'Do you live locally?'

'Yes, I do.'

'Well, I'm the licensee of the Arab Boy pub, and if you'd like to drop in one evening, it'll be drinks on the house.'

Dinsdale, always up for a free drink, accepted graciously.

'Come on Thursday, after eight o'clock.'

We said our goodbyes, and as we continued our walk, she called after us, 'Thursday's our gay night, Linsdale! You *are* gay, aren't you?'

Dinsdale swung around. 'I'm most certainly *not* gay, madam. Whatever gave you that idea?'

'I'm sorry dear, I just assumed.'

Dinsdale stomped off in a huff. I laughed.

'You may well laugh, Michael. The only reason she thought I was gay was because I was with you.'

'Me?' I said. 'What's it got to do with me?'

'Well, you're so camp, everyone thinks you're gay.'

'Oh charming, Din, many thanks.'

'No, I'm serious,' he said.

And as we walked over the common arguing, the lady publican followed our progress clearly thinking, 'a couple of old queens and no mistake'.

★ ★ ★

One evening, when Dinsdale was starring in Dennis Potter's *Sufficient Carbohydrate* at the Albery Theatre, the stage doorman rang through to his dressing room.

'There's a Mr Shenko who would love to meet you.'

'Who?' asked Dinsdale.

'He's Russian. You know, Dinsdale, he's been in the papers. He's that defective *pilot*.'

Dinsdale vaguely remembered a Soviet air force plane landing in England. When the man arrived backstage with an entourage of friends, Dinsdale regaled him with stories of his exploits in the RAF during National Service. The Russian looked bemused as he left his dressing room. Perhaps he didn't understand English very well, thought Dinsdale. He subsequently discovered that the man was in fact the political *poet* Yevgeny Yevtushenko, who had recently defected from Russia.

Laurie's client David Tomlinson was pestering him, and one thing Laurie did not like was being pestered by his clients. Ideally he would have preferred it if they didn't ring him at all, apart from the ones who worked all the time, like Larry and John and Ralph. Frances had told Mr Tomlinson that Laurie was on the other line; I'd told him that Laurie was out at a meeting; the office secretary Anne-Marie was so terrified, she had told him that Mr Evans was off sick, a rather over-dramatic invention of which Laurie would certainly not have approved.

I soon learned that agents will do almost anything to avoid talking to their clients.

He's in a meeting.

He's on the other line.

He's out of the office.

He's ill.

He's dead.

When clients ring, it inevitably leads to talking about work.

'What's happening?' the actor asks. The agent then grabs the nearest trade paper – *Variety*, *Screen International*, *Broadcast* or as a last resort *The Stage* – and rattles off lists of films, television and theatre productions, none of which the client is remotely right for; but it does show he is earning his 10 per cent, even if at present it's 10 per cent of nothing. The interview is always a good stopgap.

'Never be frightened of your clients,' Laurie told me. 'They need you more than you need them.' Some of the other agents in the office took a different view. Kenneth Carten, a sixty-five-year-old, unmarried, chain-smoking, highly strung, ex-studio talent scout, much respected in the business as he had discovered most of the film stars of the day at obscure reps and drama schools, was terrified of his clients. Whenever the telephone rang he leapt out of his chair, covering himself and everyone else in cigarette ash. I remember Kenneth once telling me: 'Get them an interview, and don't worry if they're wrong for the part. OK, they won't get the job, but at least they've had the interview and won't be able to complain that they "haven't-been-up-for-anything-for-months", well at least not for a few more months.'

The legendary actress Athene Seyler, then in her nineties, was put up for a job by Kenneth. The young director at the interview didn't know who she was.

'So tell me Athene, what have you been up to?'

'Up to?' replied Athene. 'What do you mean, this morning?'

Kenneth appeared in my office one day waving a television cast breakdown in front of me. 'There's a part here for a twenty-five-year-old French-speaking waiter,' he said, licking his lips.

'Yes?'

'Suggest Peter Sallis.'

'How old is Peter?'

'Forty.'

'But he's supposed to be twenty-five.'

'Don't worry. Peter can play younger.'

'And he speaks French?'

'No, but if they offer him the part he can always learn it. Just suggest him and for God's sake get him a meeting!'

The real problem, Kenneth told me, is when the client wants more money. 'Get me more money, but don't lose the job,' are instructions that one dreads getting from a client.

'I'm not working for *that*,' they huff and puff.

'Right, I'll try and up it, but if they won't increase their offer, shall I turn it down?'

'Oh no. I'll do it for that, but try and get some more.'

So now you start the tricky process of pretending to the producer that your client won't take the job unless he pays him more money, while knowing that the actor will do it at any price.

'He loves the part, loves the script, loves the director, the producer, the casting director. He loves everyone. It's just the money he doesn't love.'

If there really isn't any more money, and the job looks as if it might be going away from you, you can then say that, although the money stinks, he'll do it, because he loves the script, loves the part, etc. etc. etc.

The easier one, of course, is when the actor *really* won't take the job unless he's paid more money. No loving required here, just a straight 'I'm sorry, the money's shit – an insult. He's so hurt with the offer that I think he's gone off the whole idea.' Hopefully this angle will winkle out an improved offer and make the actor feel less hurt and insulted.

A lurking danger, to the negotiating skills of the agent, is if the producer goes round the back door to the actor personally, and the actor buckles under the pressure of flattery, blackmail, or whatever other angle the producer dreams up, and accepts the job. The agent then gets all the blame and the actor comes out smelling of roses, although, unfortunately, not of money.

David Tomlinson was keen to speak to his agent. Laurie said, 'See if you can help him, Michael. I'm out for the rest of the day.' I couldn't, and Tomlinson was getting agitated.

The following morning, Frances came into Laurie's room. 'It's Mr Tomlinson on the line again, Mr Evans.'

'I can't believe this. I will not be hounded by bloody David Tomlinson. Tell him I'm out of the office for the rest of the week.'

Frances returned.

'Mr Tomlinson says will you turn round and look out of the window?'

'Don't be ridiculous Frances, I'm not here. How can I look out of the window?'

'Please, Mr Evans.'

Laurie looked out of his fifth-floor window across Hanover Street to the building opposite. There, waving at Laurie, was David Tomlinson, who had asked the people in the office over the road if he could stand in the window to play a joke on a friend. David left the agency soon afterwards. Some years later, I met him at Shepperton Studios, and he mentioned that he didn't have an agent. Indeed he hadn't had one since he'd left Laurie. I was a great admirer of his work, although I'd heard that he could be *difficult*, especially when it came to money, but I thought I had nothing to lose by inviting him to lunch.

As we left the restaurant, he said, 'Well, what do you think? Would you like to be my agent?'

'Yes,' I replied, 'I think we could work very well together.'

'I agree; by the way, I don't pay commission.'

'Right,' I said. 'So what's in it for me, David?'

'Well, you'll have the prestige of having me on your books.'

'OK, David, leave that one with me.'

I left it.

Laurie had asked me to look after a famous actress of her day, who had had a brief Hollywood moment in her twenties; she was now in her mid-forties and was finding life a bit of a struggle. I couldn't get her arrested and when she asked me to have lunch with her at the Caprice, I thought the sack could be on the way.

After she'd nervously pushed a few scallops around her plate and we'd run out of small talk, she announced rather too loudly, 'I'm leaving you!'

The party at the next table stopped talking.

'I can't say I'm altogether surprised. Who are you leaving me for?'

'Jeremy Conway,' she replied.

By now we'd clearly picked up a couple of other tables, who were waiting for the next revelation.

'I should have guessed,' I replied. 'Jeremy's very good.'

'Or Joy Jameson. Having had a man looking after me, I thought perhaps I should give a woman a try.'

The restaurant was riveted.

'Joy's good too,' I said, 'but I wouldn't have thought right for you, especially if you're looking for a long-term relationship.'

The wine waiter seemed to be hovering longer than he needed to.

'Well, I wish you luck with whatever you decide, and please remember, if things don't work out with Jeremy or Joy, you can always come back to me,' I said.

When we left, I almost expected a round of applause.

It was the end of my first year at ICM, and as I was pouring myself a cup of coffee in the boardroom prior to our 11 a.m. meeting, Dick said, 'Michael, have you heard Stanley died over the weekend?'

'He was only in his sixties,' spluttered Kenneth, opening up his second cigarette pack of the day. 'No age.'

Stanley was a leading actors' agent, much respected in the business.

'Had he been ill for long?' I asked.

'No, it was all very sudden,' said Laurie. 'I'd no idea he was unwell.'

'Poor old Stanley,' said Robin.

I took a sip of coffee.

'Who did he represent?' I asked.

A loud cheer went up around the room. Bets had been laid on how long it would take between my being given the tragic news of Stanley's demise and my asking about his client list. The period of mourning had been even shorter than anyone had predicted. I had clearly come of age.

5

Hanging Fire

Our move to Grafton Street, as a result of the amalgamation of ICM and CMA, two giants of the American agency world, unfortunately slid me down several rungs of the ladder, just as I was slowly making my way up it. Despite my having being groomed by Laurie Evans as the heir apparent, a number of CMA agents seemed to have bigger desks than mine; I was beginning to wonder whether it was time for me to move on. My salary was stuck somewhere between that of Laurie's chauffeur and the office bookkeeper, and Laurie inspected my monthly expenses like a vulture poring over a carcass.

I was, however, continuing to take on new clients – mostly my colleagues' cast-offs. The film director Roy Ward Baker was passed to me by Dick Blodget. Roy had been a major director in the 1950s – the *Titanic* film, *A Night to Remember*, was one of his triumphs – but by the 1970s he'd been overtaken by a rash of younger directors, and had now started to specialize in low-budget horror films such as *Taste the Blood of Dracula* and *The Vampire Lovers*. He had been invited to the Sitges Film Festival of Fantasy and Horror. As there were two tickets available and Roy's partner was unavailable, I joined him for an all-expenses-paid junket to Spain.

We left London early in the morning and arrived at Gatwick to discover that our pre-paid tickets were not at the BA desk. Anxious to get on with our journey, we paid for the tickets ourselves and arrived at Barcelona Airport a couple of hours later. The chauffeur-driven limousine, which was supposed to be waiting for us at the airport, failed to materialize, so we took a cab for the twenty-mile trip to Sitges. We arrived at our hotel just in time for our lunch with one of the festival organizers. Unfortunately, the hotel had no reservations for our two-night stay, but was able to offer us two tiny single rooms for which we had to pay in advance on *my* credit card; one overlooked the car park and the other the hotel laundry.

We had a collection time of 12.45 p.m. on our itinerary, but as nobody had arrived by 1.15, we took a cab to the restaurant. We gave the name of our hostess to the maître d', who knew the lady but had no reservation for her, and regretted that the restaurant was fully booked. By now, Roy was feeling neglected and unloved.

'What shall we do?' he asked.

'Get on the next plane home?' I suggested. At which point a classy-looking brunette grabbed Roy's hand.

'Ah, Mr Baker,' she gushed, 'Marian Carrero from the festival committee. Please forgive me for being so late. Let's have lunch.'

Unfortunately Miss Carrero was unable to twist the maître d's arm so we walked up the street to a deserted pizzeria, where Marian ordered the lightest of lunches. She informed us of the evening's arrangements: pick up at 6.45 p.m., black tie, drinks party at the Hilton for guests of the festival and fellow judges, followed by dinner.

Christopher Lee and Peter Cushing, who happened to be two old friends of Roy, would be there. Things were now looking up. Marian glanced at her watch: it was three o'clock; she had to be at the airport by four to meet Max Von Sydow. She dashed.

'See you later, darlings,' she shouted as she swept out of the restaurant, leaving me to pick up the bill.

Back at our hotel, we had time to bathe and change, ready for collection at 6.45. By 7.15 nobody had arrived, and the twenty-four-hour manned contact number Marian had given me in case of emergency was on an answering machine in Spanish. We took a cab to the Hilton and waited patiently in a queue of 'celebrity' guests.

'Bakkar? No Bakkar on the list,' said the girl on the door. 'You Brooker?'

'No, Roy Ward Baker,' said Roy, 'and Michael Whitehall.'

'No Whyhole here either,' she said. 'A minute please, you stand aside.'

Having waited for fifteen minutes while assorted guests including Max Von Sydow were ushered into the ballroom, Roy recognized someone in the queue.

'Michael!' he called. It was Michael Carreras, son of the founder of Hammer Films, Sir James Carreras.

'Roy, what are you doing here?'

Roy explained.

'Sorry, mate. It's all a bit chaotic. You know the Spanish.'

'You know this Bakkar?' said the girl at the desk. 'And this Whyhole?'

Michael nodded and we were in. He then dashed off to join his party, leaving Roy and me to wander around the ballroom, sipping warm Frexinet. We knew nobody. No Marian, no Christopher Lee, no Peter Cushing; even Max Von Sydow seemed to have been whisked away to some *salon privé*.

Dinner was announced, and as we crowded around the board showing the table plan, we found neither a 'Bakkar' nor a 'Whyhole'. Max Von Sydow seemed to have got himself neatly tucked in at the top table next to a couple of Spanish starlets – no such luck for Roy and me. That was it.

As the guests filed into dinner we strode out of the ballroom, swept past the girl on the door, who by now was attempting to control an irate queue of unlisted guests, hailed a cab, collected our things from the hotel, paid the bill and headed for the airport.

'How was Sitges?' asked Dick Blodget the following day. 'You're back early.'

'Not a huge success to be honest, Dick,' I replied.

'One of our clients was presenting an award. Did you see him?'

'Who was that, Dick?' I asked.

'Max Von Sydow.'

Later Dick passed me a letter from a Mr Scott Schukat of the Schukat Corporation in New York. At the head of the page was the company's logo: a cat playing with a shoe. Neat, I thought. Mr Schukat was a personal manager and one of his clients was the totally unknown (certainly to me, in any case) Northern J. Calloway. Mr Calloway was a client of ICM in New York and was about to arrive in London for the musical *Pippin*; and I should 'extend all courtesies' to him. Having just suffered a severe bout of discourtesy in Spain, I thought I'd be especially charming to Mr Calloway.

He appeared in my office a few days later, a diffident black man of about twenty-five, pleasant and shy, unlike his manager, who flew into town a few days later, in time for the opening night. He burst through my door, all five feet five inches of him, like a mini-Superman. Had I fixed up any meetings for Northern? He should see all the top producers, directors, casting directors. What about films?

I suggested that perhaps we should wait until the show had opened. At the time nobody knew who he was. He had also told me that Northern was 'starring' in the show, which wasn't totally accurate.

'You just wait, Michael. After tomorrow night people will be stepping off the sidewalk when Northern walks down the street.'

The first night went well, and Northern's performance was received enthusiastically. As I arrived at his dressing-room door, I was surprised to find it locked. I knocked, and Mr Schukat shot his head around the door and beckoned me in. The room was empty, apart from a large table covered with champagne bottles, glasses and a huge tray of canapés. Northern was standing in the corner taking off his trousers.

'Hi, Michael,' said Northern.

'Well done, Northern. Great performance,' I replied.

'More than great,' said Scott. 'We've got a star on our hands, Mike. A huge great eighteen-carat gold fucking star. OK, let 'em in!'

I opened the dressing-room door, and three people walked into the room. One was Northern's dresser, the other two Mr Schukat's sister and her husband. Ten minutes later, he started putting away the champagne and canapés.

'I'll call you tomorrow,' he said.

Unfortunately, the following day Northern was mentioned only in a couple of notices; the show received a mixed reception from the critics, despite our having what Schukat called 'a star on our hands'.

Northern was able to continue walking down the sidewalk without pedestrians throwing themselves into the gutter.

Kenneth More was filming the television series 'Father Brown' for Lew Grade, and I was asked to join Kenny for lunch at the ATV Studios at Elstree where he was meeting a journalist from the *News of the World*.

'Keep Kenny off the sauce,' said Laurie, 'at least until he's finished the interview, and don't let him get into too much personal stuff.'

The interview went well and Kenny avoided all the awkward questions and kept off the wine and the personal stuff. I thought I'd done my chaperoning duties to perfection. After lunch I had to get back to the office for a meeting, and the reporter walked me to the car park.

'What a charming bloke,' he said. 'Shame they're not all that nice.'

The following Sunday, I had a call from Tim Wilson, an agent at the office. 'Have you seen the *News of the World*?' he asked.

I hadn't.

He read me selected gory details: 'FATHER BROWN'S CHILLY WILLY . . . ICE COLD DOUCHES FOR TV PRIEST . . . Actor Kenneth More is using a controversial new treatment to activate his sperm in an attempt to get his new young wife pregnant.' A two-page spread of stills from the series with Kenny in costume was accompanied by diagrams of the cold-water treatment. I called Kenny, who had just seen the paper and was in shock. Apparently, after I'd left the reporter in the car park, he'd gone back to the restaurant and spotted Kenny in the bar. Kenny had been released early from filming and decided to have a quick one before returning home. The reporter offered him a drink, and after a couple more the conversation got round to his private life. (Reporters, especially show-business ones, find talking to actors about their careers deadly boring. It's their private lives they want to get into.)

'Angela wants a baby, but it's proving jolly difficult,' he said. 'Something to do with my sperm being lazy. Anyway the latest idea is that I hang my balls in cold water and try to razz them up – it all sounds pretty unlikely to me but I'm giving it a try.'

Kenny had, of course, assumed that the interview had finished at the end of lunch, and he was just having a social drink with the reporter. Lew Grade was furious. 'There's no such thing as a social drink with a reporter. Where the hell were *you*?' he shouted. 'Kenny needed protecting. You've wrecked my series!'

'Sorry, darling,' said Kenny later, 'I'll remember next time.'

★   ★   ★

Someone else who was no stranger to the occasional social drink was Trevor Howard. He once told me how he had outwitted the Thames Constabulary. He was caught driving on the M4, having had a few too many cocktails before lunch, and consequently lost his licence for a year. The police were clearly delighted to have netted such a prize catch; better still, the same police car was driving through Windsor a couple of weeks later and spotted Trevor climbing unsteadily into the driving seat of a large Mercedes with blacked-out windows. Once the car had joined a tailback on the motorway, the police pulled it over on to the hard shoulder. Trevor staggered out of the car and reluctantly agreed to take a breathalyser test, which naturally proved to be positive.

'Driving whilst disqualified is serious enough,' said the police officer, 'but being drunk as well. They'll throw the book at you.'

Trevor was invited to sit in the back of the police car on the journey to the station.

'Keys in the car, old boy,' said Trevor.

The police officer walked back to Trevor's car, opened the door. No steering wheel. He looked ahead of him and there was a uniformed chauffeur — it was a left-hand-drive car.

'He's quite a card that Mr Howard, isn't he, Officer?' said the chauffeur.

David Hemmings asked Kenny More and me to a film shoot in Berlin. David was wearing his director's hat for

Just a Gigolo, starring David Bowie and Marlene Dietrich. Unfortunately Miss Dietrich and Mr Bowie fell out with one another; so Hemmings, always the master of invention (he was a member of the Magic Circle), had to film their scenes separately: Dietrich's in Paris, where she lived, and Bowie's in Berlin.

When they were filming scenes together, body doubles had to be used and an intimate scene where they embraced needed all Hemmings's directorial guile. It was bizarre watching a scene where two actors were speaking passionately to one another in a bedroom knowing that one was in Berlin and the other in Paris.

The first evening we were there, the two Davids suggested that we hit the red-light district after dinner. The first club required us to take off all our clothes and chase naked girls around the rooms. The sight of a man with a withered arm mounting a large Asian lady with enormous breasts put us all off the idea, although I think Hemmings might have been up for it.

'I'm sorry but I'm not taking my clothes off,' said Kenny. So we moved on to the next club, strongly recommended by the doorman and not requiring guests to undress.

The Galaxy Club offered debauchery on a scale I was unaware existed. A huge room was filled with sprawling men and women in various stages of undress. The two Davids, Kenny and I were shown to a corner table where the obligatory bottles of champagne were waiting for us. The maître d' then explained the various charges, which slightly took the edge off the evening from my point of view. Four undressed young ladies joined us. The two Davids swiftly disappeared, having been offered services upstairs. Kenny was having a discussion about his film career with a topless girl sitting on his crotch. She was particularly interested in his Douglas Bader role in *Reach for the Sky*, which she had recently seen with her mother, and was reassured to discover that Kenny's legs were in good working order, as indeed were the other parts of his anatomy. They then disappeared. I was left, fully dressed in my pinstripe suit with a large, heavy-breasted naked woman sitting on my lap. As luck would have it, she didn't speak any English, but realizing that I wasn't planning to head upstairs with her, she disappeared and returned with a vibrator. She then sat on the table and started it up. A queue of eager punters quickly formed and I watched in pop-eyed astonishment at this bizarre spectacle. What was I doing at two o'clock in the morning on the fringes of an orgy?

After what seemed like an eternity, Kenny returned and asked for everyone's bill, which he duly paid. He wouldn't tell me how much it was, but I later discovered that it was well over a thousand pounds. We then made our way back to the hotel, having left the two Davids upstairs.

'I gather you and Kenny tried to lead David astray last night,' said Mrs Hemmings, who was visiting the set the following day, 'but he was a good boy.'

'Of course he was, darling,' said Kenny.

★   ★   ★

'I was left with a large, heavy-breasted naked woman
sitting on my lap'

Kenny's personal taste in nightlife was at the milder end of the scale. A favourite was the Gaslight Club, just off Jermyn Street, where topless girls would chat to punters over a bottle or two of champagne. Kenny had a soft spot for the Gaslight girls.

'Most of them are nurses on low incomes, or students working their way through college,' he would say.

The chat was often more to do with which late bus they got back to Sidcup after work, rather than anything of an erotic nature and there was a strictly no-hanky-panky policy in operation, well not on the premises anyway.

Once, when Kenny was starring in Frederick Lonsdale's *On Approval* with Moray Watson, he invited Moray and me to join him at the club after the show. Moray was a very reluctant Gaslight punter and would have much preferred to have caught the last train from Charing Cross to Etchingham in Sussex where he lived. Kenny left us in the bar while he organized a table. Into the bar came a naked Amazon wearing a shiny pink wig with her muscular arms locked around two rather nervous-looking Japanese businessmen.

'I don't think *she's* working her way through college,' said Moray.

Soon after the play finished, I fixed Moray up with a couple of days' filming in the Borders, and he had arranged to stay on the Saturday night with friends of friends before driving back to London. He completed his scenes on the Saturday morning but got lost between his hotel and the film unit base, and managed to miss breakfast at both locations. Released at midday, he decided to join his hosts for lunch at their house an hour's drive away, rather than lunching on the set. Unfortunately Moray got lost again. When he arrived, the place was deserted apart from a gardener, who told him that lunch was up the hill, where the shoot was in progress. As Moray headed up the hill, he nearly collided with a van coming down the hill with the lunch things.

'Sorry, Moray, you've just missed lunch,' said his host. 'Do you still want to shoot?'

Moray felt that he'd done quite enough shooting for one day, and as it was nearly three o'clock and he hadn't eaten anything for eighteen hours, he decided to drive to the local village for supplies. Saturday afternoon wasn't a good time for open shops in Foggorig, and he headed back to the house disappointed and famished. By the time he'd found the house again, the tea things had been removed and the butler was laying up for dinner.

He tried to take his mind off food and went for a walk around the estate. After a bath and a change, he heard the welcoming sound of the dinner gong and almost knocked over one of his fellow guests in his unseemly rush to get into the drawing room for cocktails. The last thing he wanted was a cocktail, but a cheese straw or a crisp he would have killed for. Sadly none was in evidence.

As he walked through to the dining room with his hearty hostess she announced, 'This is really more of a supper, Moray. When we have a shoot everyone eats far too much at lunchtime, and I think it's rather unfair forcing more food down them in the evening. But we'll have a huge lunch tomorrow.'

'Actually I'm leaving for London first thing in the morning, but don't worry, I'm a terribly light eater.'

It certainly was 'more of a supper': a small piece of rather dry cod, a couple of sprigs of broccoli and three new potatoes, which he gobbled down so quickly he nearly choked on them. There was also a tiny jelly with a dab of cream on it; and as he was dreaming about a non-existent cheese board with chunks of local cheddar and slices of crusty bread, everyone was ushered through to the library for coffee. Moray's eyes shot hungrily around the room, looking for mints or other after-dinner delicacies; it was a vain quest.

Everyone was tired after a day's shooting and an early night was decreed. As he started to mount the staircase with his host, Moray noticed, through the kitchen door, sitting on the table, a large chocolate gateau with a couple of slices removed, presumably having made an earlier appearance at the shoot. As he worked out how many slices he'd be able to cut off the cake without anyone noticing, and whether he should come downstairs still dressed or in his dressing gown and slippers, his host said, 'Not planning to go downstairs again tonight, are you Moray?'

'No, absolutely not,' he spluttered. Had he been thinking aloud?

'Good,' replied his host, as he pressed a selection of buttons on the wall. 'I've set the alarm system, which covers the lower part of the house. It's bloody sensitive and the police are round here like a shot if it's activated. Sleep well.'

Being round famous people is a strange and rather surreal experience. You go to a bar or restaurant with a well-known face and the maître d' and his staff are all over you like a cheap suit. Fawning on an Olympian scale is followed by that forced intimacy that people, particularly those in the catering industry, like to affect.

'You'd probably like to look at the wine list, Sir Trevor,' says the sommelier. Does he know something about Sir Trevor's drinking habits that we don't?

'I've put a lobster aside for you, Mr Griffiths. Just in case.'

'Your usual table, Dame Dorothy?' asks the maître d'.

'I have never been here before,' she whispers as he goes off to get the menu.

But when I return to the restaurant with my doctor, the maître d' ignores me, the lobster's off and I've got that table right between the ladies' room and the waiters' serving station.

One restaurant where I always got a warm welcome was Macready's, a popular theatrical haunt in Covent Garden.

I went there once shortly after seeing Stewart Granger in Spain, when he had spoken fondly about his ex-wives Jean Simmons and Elspeth March. I didn't know Elspeth personally but spotted her at a table with a group of friends. Introducing myself to strangers has never been my forte, which is why I was such a slow study in poaching other agents' clients; but this seemed like a good opportunity to pass on the warmth of her husband's feelings towards her.

'Excuse me, may I introduce myself?'

The lady gave me a hesitant smile. Maybe she thought that I was after her autograph and didn't have any paper.

'I'm Michael Whitehall, and I've just been with Jimmy Granger in Marbella,' I said brightly.

She looked blank.

'He spoke so fondly of you and I thought I must just say hello.'

More blank stares from her and the rest of her party. I ploughed on.

'You are Elspeth March, aren't you?' I said, sensing that I may have put my foot into something.

'No, I'm most certainly not,' the woman replied, clearly very annoyed.

At which point I had a much-needed flash of inspiration. Of course, I knew who this was, and, of course, she wasn't Elspeth March. What was I doing in the middle of a crowded restaurant, causing acute embarrassment not only to myself but to this total stranger? Thank God, I was able to get out of this one. This wasn't Elspeth March: this was Brian Rix's wife, the actress Elspet Gray, whom I also had never met.

'I'm so sorry,' I blustered. 'Of course you're not Elspeth March, you're Elspet Gray!'

The woman gave me a long and contemptuous stare.

'I'm neither Elspeth fucking March nor Elspet fucking Gray. I'm Margaret fucking Courtenay. Now kindly get out of my fucking way.'

When I was flying to Australia with Kenny More to the première of a film called *The Slipper and the Rose*, which he made in the late 1970s, we flew first class. En route to Sydney, the plane stopped in Bahrain. Sitting in the lounge, Kenny was approached by a German couple.

'We know you,' the man said.

Kenny smiled.

'You actor famous.'

'Thank you, darling,' said Kenny and went back to his newspaper as the couple wandered off.

Later in the flight, when Kenny was fast asleep, they reappeared and shook him by the shoulder.

'We know you. You from *Reach the Sky*. You Barder!'

Kenny gave them a bleary smile – it was, after all, the middle of the night.

'Can we have autograph?'

'Of course, darling,' Kenny replied. 'You have pen and paper?'

'No pen, no paper,' they said. Why don't people asking for autographs ever have pens or paper handy? Kenny rootled around in his bag, found a pen and a pad and duly autographed it for them. Off they went, peering at the paper: they clearly had no idea who Kenny was.

A few hours later, I was talking to the steward. 'Mr More is so charming. Those people had no business waking him up,' he said. 'Very different from the gentleman we had on this flight last week,' he added.

'Who was that?' I asked.

'Frank Sinatra on his way to a concert in Sydney.'

'What happened?' I asked.

'Well, this young boy, Japanese I think he was, walked into first class to Mr Sinatra's seat. He was looking at some papers and didn't see the boy. The boy then asked very politely if he could have his autograph. Sinatra turned towards him, gave him a withering look, and said, "Pen and paper?" The boy obliged. When Sinatra handed him back the paper, he'd written "Fuck off, you prick" and hadn't even signed it.'

I think if I had been woken up by a couple of Germans in the middle of the night I might have done it Frank's way.

Meanwhile in Grafton Street, I was beginning to tread water, which, going by my previous history, did not bode well. Laurie had often spoken to me of promotion once he had retired, but a long wait in the wings didn't appeal. (Laurie remained an agent until he was well into his eighties, so it would have been a very long wait.) I had also failed to get a decent pay rise: I now had a large office and a small salary, but I would have preferred it the other way around. I didn't think I had the bottle, or indeed the money, to set up my own agency, so I started looking around for a suitable partner. I met several agents who were keen on the idea but unfortunately the feeling was not mutual. In fact the more agents I met, the more I wondered whether I should just stick it out with Laurie.

'You're just the partner I've been waiting for all my life,' said a middle-aged, suspiciously ginger-haired agent who was clearly uninhibited when it came to facial enhancement. After a very hot lunch at his local Indian restaurant his mascara began to run, giving him the look of Dirk Bogarde in *Death in Venice*. When we arrived back at his office, just off Regent Street, he slumped into an armchair and started to cry. 'It's very lonely working on your own,' he said, 'but I used to enjoy it when I was younger.' He then started to list all the clients who had left him as well as the few who had remained, including the six-times-married Hedy Lamarr, whom he claimed to represent 'in the UK only'. I couldn't wait to leave his stuffy office and get back to the air-conditioned delights of 22 Grafton Street.

Another agent, with a long and fairly classy client list, suggested we meet up at his local pub, which happened to be near my house. He and his business partner were in the middle of an acrimonious split, and he didn't think that the office would be the most harmonious of locations for a meeting.

'I've got all the good clients and he's got all the rubbish, but he thinks we should split everything fifty-fifty. No way.'

He seemed very angry with life and the more gin and tonics he drank, the angrier he became.

'You've got class, Michael, just like me,' he said, crunching on a mouthful of peanuts. 'He wouldn't know class if it was shoved into his face. You only need to look at his list. You wouldn't catch me representing Cardew Robinson.'

Rather embarrassingly he started, in far too loud a voice, discussing money with me.

'What are you earning at the moment, Michael? Nothing, I bet. I know what Laurie pays – fuck all.'

'Well, not . . .'

'I could guarantee you ten thousand pounds per annum, plus a share of the profits.' (This was more than double what I was earning at ICM.) 'And make you a partner.'

Like a bad date, this was all moving too quickly. I'd met this chap only an hour before and he was almost proposing marriage. He also seemed to be including most of the lounge bar regulars in the conversation.

'How soon could you spring yourself out of Laurie's clutches?' he shouted.

'Well, obviously, I've got to think it over. But it's clearly worth us talking more about later.'

'What more is there to talk about? I'm up for it. How many of Laurie's clients will you be able to poach? Olivier wouldn't be easy, but Gielgud and Richardson must be ready for a change. Have another G&T?'

This man was completely mad and also on his way to becoming completely drunk.

'I've got to dash, but let's talk on the telephone,' I said. 'I'll call you tomorrow.' This, of course, I didn't do. I took the coward's way out and wrote and told him that Laurie had agreed to double my salary, give me a share of the profits, make me a director of the company and sit on top of my tree at Christmas.

A colleague at ICM, with some decent clients, was keen to leave with me, which I thought was the perfect solution. Unfortunately, he had a severe attack of cold feet when the prospect of being sued by Laurie was raised.

And then I met Julian Belfrage . . .

6

The Dilettantes of St James's

In the old days, agents were the butt of music hall jokes, characterised as ill-bred, barely literate low-lifers, working out of grubby one-room offices on the Charing Cross Road. Their American counterparts were usually portrayed in movies as dishonest, overweight, cigar-chomping wide boys. Julian was as far a cry from these two stereotypes as it was possible to be, apart perhaps from the odd cigar. Brown trilby hat (from Locks, of course), covert coat, grey suit, Turnbull & Asser shirt and an old school tie constituted his uniform. (At weekends a pair of binoculars around his neck and a racing badge were added to this get-up.) Good-looking in a 'hooray' kind of way, with thinning hair and piercing blue eyes, Julian had been working for Terence Plunkett Greene for some years and was also looking for a change in direction.

We had a couple of meetings in a pub in Albemarle Street, and then Julian asked me to lunch with Terry Plunkett Greene at the Turf Club. This came as a surprise: my interest in working with Julian didn't extend to Mr Plunkett Greene.

'A very good afternoon to you, sir,' said Mr Plunkett Greene as I walked into the bar. 'You must be Mr Whitehall?'

In front of me, clutching a gin and tonic, stood this middle-aged dandy. He was wearing a bottle-green tweed suit with velvet collar, a silk tie with a pearl tie pin, a red pocket handkerchief, spats and, attached precariously to his right eye, a monocle; an upmarket version of ventriloquist Ray Alan's dummy, Lord Charles.

Terry was, however, no dummy. Charming and articulate, he was an agent very much of the old school, but absolutely not the casting I envisaged for our new agency. Their proposal was that Julian and I would be directors of the new company, and Terry would be chairman. The unwieldy name of 'Plunkett Greene, Belfrage & Whitehall' was suggested, and their existing offices in Jermyn Street were offered as the company's new premises. None of which appealed to me at all. I had a vision of a new, thrusting theatrical agency, which would attract the *crème de la crème* of acting talent, offering superlative pastoral management, a service our larger and more powerful rivals would be unable to match. But what I seemed to be walking into was a team of time-warped 'hooray Henrys' who looked as though they'd be more at home in the winner's enclosure at Sandown Park than at the BAFTA Awards. But looks can be deceptive, and in Julian's case they certainly deceived me. I learned more about agents and agency from him than from anyone else, and I have many reasons to be grateful to him.

I never got that far with Terry. I told Julian after our meeting that if we were going to move forward together, it would have to be without Terry. It took Julian some time to mull over this. After a few days, he finally telephoned me to say that Terry had agreed to step aside. We now needed premises. Walking down St James's Street from ICM's offices in Grafton Street to meet Julian at the Turf Club, I noticed a 'To Let' sign opposite Boodle's at number 60.

'We couldn't possibly afford it,' I said to Julian over lunch. We had put together a bank overdraft to set up the new business, which we had decided to call 'Leading Artists'. I didn't like Belfrage & Whitehall, never having been keen on second billing, and thought that Leading Artists had a certain ring to it. LA also seemed an appropriate pair of initials and if we expanded, as I hoped we would, we would not need to add names every couple of years, ending up as Belfrage, Whitehall, Weinstein, Goslett & Marks, or whatever. No, Leading Artists sounded like a class act, which indeed it turned out to be, despite a few hiccoughs along the way.

'I'll do some research,' said Julian. 'I know someone at the estate agents. He's a keen racing man; we both had legs of a horse once. Cost us a bloody fortune.'

Julian telephoned the following day. 'A bit of luck on that office in St James's Street; it's owned by Mark Furness, who happens to live on the top floor.' Mark Furness was a theatrical producer, specializing in tours. Although Julian and I had spoken to him from time to time, we had never met. After an early-evening drink, we decided to cold-call him. He ushered us into his top-floor apartment, and Julian gave him our hard-luck story.

Furness was a huge bear of a man, permanently covered in cigar ash, with a white pasty complexion; he looked as though he should get out more. He was also clearly the worse for wear in the cocktail department. Julian tried to get the conversation round to the touring business.

'The Yvonne Arnaud in Guildford is a good-looking theatre, isn't it?' he said. 'How many does it seat?'

'I've no idea,' replied Furness.

'Do you have anything in the pipeline at the moment?' I enquired.

'No,' came the curt reply.

'I really enjoyed the tour of *Don't Just Lie There, Say Something!*. Michael Pertwee is such a subtle writer,' schmoozled Julian. 'Now that must have done some business.'

Furness went to pour himself another brandy.

'Julian, I don't think this is Mark Furness,' I whispered. 'He doesn't seem to have heard of *any* of these plays; and I think Mark is much younger.'

'Are you still planning to do *Who Goes Bare?* this Christmas?' Julian kept going.

'I'm spending Christmas in the Canaries,' said Furness.

Mark Furness presented a string of pantomimes over Christmas, and it seemed odd that he was planning to be in the Canaries at such a busy time of year.

Julian then told Furness that we were planning to set up a theatrical agency and needed an office in the area, but that, due to our limited funds, we couldn't afford the rent.

'I'm a great fan of the theatrical world,' he slurred. 'Lost quite a bit on investing in plays, but still go on doing it. Don't see why I shouldn't invest in you two by letting you have the second floor at a tolerable rent. I actually own the whole building through our family trust, so I'm allowed to be philanthropic from time to time.'

This man was beginning to sound less and less like Mark Furness, king of the tatty tours.

'Here's my card. Give me a call next week, and I'll have the estate agent show you round the office.'

As we hit the cold night air of St James's and staggered into the back of a cab, full of Furness's brandy and cigar smoke, we looked at his card – 'Viscount Furness'.

Back at the Turf Club, we opened *Who's Who* – 'William Anthony Furness, 2nd Viscount. Son of 1st Viscount and Thelma . . .'

'Illegitimate son of Edward VIII and Thelma Furness, I believe,' said Julian's friend Knut Robson. 'But don't quote me. Bloody loaded.'

So far so good: Julian had sorted out his exit from Plunkett Greene, and we now had a set of smart premises. Unfortunately, I now had to extract myself from ICM.

I went to see Laurie after one of our eleven o'clock meetings, and told him that I'd decided to leave ICM and set up my own agency with Julian.

'Hopeless agent,' said Laurie, 'I sacked him twice at MCA. Couldn't run a bath. But if you've made your mind up.'

I had. Laurie asked me when I was planning to go.

'I thought at the end of the month, if that's all right with you?'

'Would lunchtime suit?' said Laurie.

When I returned to my office, after a quick meeting with Julian in Jermyn Street, my desk had been cleared, and a hand-delivered letter was waiting for me from ICM's lawyers. A particularly elegant Victorian button-back chair which I had used during my time at the agency, and which I had coveted as a memento of my time there, had also been removed. No mention of furniture, but the letter warned me that if I took any of ICM's clients with me, legal proceedings would be instigated against me.

True to his word, Laurie had me up before the beak within a few days. My solicitor, the urbane Brook Land, assured me there was very little chance of ICM securing an injunction against me for reasons of restrictions of trade, unfair competition and various other things, none of which I really understood. Nabarro Nathanson was a top firm of solicitors, so I was in safe hands. They retained a bright young barrister by the name of Anthony Grabiner (now Lord Grabiner), with whom I had a very brief meeting before the hearing. Unfortunately, he had a streaming cold and was losing his voice.

'You sound and look terrible, Tony,' said Brook.

'Yes, I think I've got a temperature, so don't come too near. Who's the judge?'

'Sidney Templeman.'

'Damn, used to be a commercial lawyer, not a supporter of the little man against the big conglomerate. Well, we'll do our best,' he spluttered.

'Mr Whitehall is attempting to steal some of ICM's leading clients; clients contracted to my client as clients,' Laurie's barrister told the court.

Rather too many clients in that sentence, I thought.

'Can you give me some names?' asked Mr Justice Templeman.

Mr Potter – I believe that was his name – had to refer to his notes as he clearly couldn't remember any of them. 'Umm . . . D-Doug . . . F-Fisher, my lord,' he stuttered, 'L-Linsdale Danden.'

'Indeed,' said Templeman.

'Robin Hawdon, Jeremy Child, Sheila Davies,' he continued, having got the hang of it.

151

Mr Justice Templeman's eyes were beginning to glaze over.

'And, of course, Kenneth More, my lord.'

'Ah, Kenneth More,' said Mr Justice Templeman, perking up. *'Reach for the Clouds.'*

'Ermm . . . *Sky*, my lord,' said the ever-helpful Mr Potter.

'I'm obliged, Mr Potter.'

At this point Mr Grabiner had a sneezing fit. 'My apologies, my lord.'

'A touch of flu, Mr Grabiner?'

'I think so, my lord.'

Well, they seem to be getting on OK, I thought.

'I have been told by prosecuting counsel that Mr Whitehall took a number of ICM's major clients,' asked the judge.

'I don't believe so, my lord,' said Grabiner.

'This list includes actors such as Jeremy Child, Robin Hawdon and Doug Fisher. All important actors, contributing considerable agency fees to ICM.'

I waited for Grabiner to tell Mr Templeman that ICM's clients included John Gielgud, Albert Finney, Peter Finch, Laurence Olivier, Rex Harrison, Vanessa Redgrave and Ralph Richardson, and Messrs Child, Hawdon and Fisher's earnings wouldn't have covered their taxi fares. But no.

'Indeed, my lord, but . . .' and so it went on. The point had been missed. The judge had made up his mind and ICM obtained their injunction. So much for restriction of trade. No agency had ever received an injunction against a departing agent before, and, as far as I know, none has since.

Julian was very understanding; so too were my clients; and, to my surprise, so was Laurie.

'I gather all your clients are leaving us. To be honest we wouldn't have wanted most of them anyway, although I was very surprised Kenny went with you after all I've done for him.' Why was Laurie ringing me, I wondered?

'By the terms of the injunction, they can, of course, go to any agency in London, apart from this set-up that you and Belfrage are planning to run.'

'Will be running, Laurie,' I said.

'Well anyway, if we can come to some arrangement regarding the commission, then I might agree to vary the injunction.'

The penny dropped. Why was I so slow when it came to big business and high finance? The following day, Laurie's solicitors wrote to Brook proposing that, provided I paid ICM 10 per cent commission on all their contracts for a three-year period, I could represent the agreed list of clients. Brook cleverly got it down to two years, and all my actors agreed to pay 15 per cent for that period, so at least there was a bit of income coming into the business from my side. But by the time we'd agreed to pay Laurie all my commission for two years, paid the legal costs, put down a deposit on our new office in St James's and arranged a bank loan, the future started to look a bit bleak.

A month or so later we opened for business at 60 St James's Street. I was told that two agents had been discussing our arrival into the theatrical market-place. Would their clients be safe from our blandishments? 'Nothing to fear from them,' said the agent, Jeremy Conway, 'they're just a couple of socialite dilettantes.'

Julian was furious when he heard this story, I less so; indeed I was quite flattered that we were even being talked about. When I spoke to Julian about it, he cut me short: '*Socialite* dilettantes? Oh, that's OK. I thought you said *socialist*.'

Julian already had an impressive list of actors: Colin Blakely, Ian Holm, John Hurt, Daniel Massey, David Warner, Judi Dench, Virginia McKenna – and we were soon taking on new clients. The business began to grow.

I built up my list with some talented young and not so young actors: Richard Griffiths, Colin Firth, John Wells, Tom Courtenay, Donald Sinden, Maria Aitken, Edward Fox, Peter Bowles, Keith Barron, Nigel Havers, Ian Charleson, David Hemmings, James Fox and John Le Mesurier. Richard Cottrell, a director client of Julian's, urged us to come and see a very clever young actor at

Bristol. It wasn't a wasted visit: Daniel Day-Lewis was a wonderful new client for us.

There were a few, however, that didn't make the cut. In the mid-1970s, Sir Michael Havers, who at the time was Attorney General, asked me whether I would meet his friend Jeffrey Archer. Jeffrey burst into my office like a tornado and, after much hand-shaking, pressed a bulky envelope into my arms.

'Read this and let me know what you think,' he said. 'I've written a book.'

It was a proof copy of Jeffrey's first book, *Not a Penny More, Not a Penny Less*, but that wasn't the point of Jeffrey's visit.

'I want to play James Bond,' he said, 'and you can get it for me.'

What an invitation! I asked Jeffrey what acting experience he had had.

'None,' he replied, 'but I know I can do it.'

At the time, Jeffrey was in his early forties and I suggested that he'd left an acting career a bit late in the day.

'I don't want an acting career, I just want to play James Bond.'

In fact, the Bond people were looking for someone to take over from Roger Moore – Timothy Dalton ultimately got the part – so I promised to look into it for him.

I then flicked through the galley proofs of his book.

'This looks interesting. Have you got a book agent?'

'Yes I have,' said Jeffrey. 'I just need you to look after my acting.'

Fortunately, when the book was published to great acclaim, Jeffrey put his acting aspirations on hold, although he did subsequently tread the boards in his play *The Accused*. And indeed he has been no stranger to a spot of play-acting in other departments.

Julian was a great stickler for form, and not just the racing kind. He introduced Adam Ant to me as 'Mr Ant' and Ringo Starr as 'Mr Starr'. We represented them for a brief time, both with very limited success. Ringo was the only client I ever had who would never come to my office; I always had to go to his. A status thing I guess. Come to think of it, my other pop-star client Bob Geldof wouldn't come to the office either. Maybe it's a music thing.

'Good morning to you, sir,' was Julian's common mode of greeting on the telephone. A seventeen-year-old secretary, ringing to check an actor's availability for a voice-over, would be asked: 'Are you in good order, ma'am?' And then Julian would get down to business. He could be fiercely protective of his clients. 'Bisto? John Hurt doesn't advertise gravy. Don't you know who he is?' '*Fourth* billing did you say? Judi Dench didn't get an OBE for cooking, you know,' he told a film producer, trying to sort out a difficult billing problem. 'He might well be a bigger name than Judi, but unfortunately, as everyone knows apart from you, he can't do it.' He always had very clear-cut views on the performances he saw. 'The worst performance I have ever seen on a professional stage,' was a fairly regular response from Julian after an evening at the theatre. 'The sooner he realizes that he can't act, the better!' He could get very cross with me if I didn't watch his clients either on film or on television, and more especially on stage.

'Bob Lang is giving the best performance of any actor in any medium I have ever seen. You must go and see it. But hurry up, it comes off on Saturday.' ·

'Where's it on, Julian?'

'The Studio at the Haymarket Theatre in Leicester.'

And when I didn't go, 'Bob was very upset. You missed one of the best . . .'

Of course, Bob wasn't remotely upset, it was Julian he wanted to see, not me.

Julian liked to take clients to the Turf Club, provided that they were properly dressed in a suit and tie, which of course they seldom were. Shortly after we had taken him on, we asked Peter Bowles to lunch. Julian booked the Turf Club, but in case of dress problems also booked Langan's Brasserie, a regular haunt of ours.

Peter arrived in our office elegantly dressed in a pale-blue suit, silk shirt and tie – the full business. As we walked downstairs and into St James's Street, I whispered to Julian, 'Turf Club?'

'Langan's,' he replied.

'Langan's?' I said. 'But he's immaculate.'

'He may be immaculate but he's carrying a handbag!'

I hadn't noticed Peter's small, black purse, containing presumably his gentleman's cologne and other travelling essentials.

'Have you ever seen a man at the Turf Club carrying a handbag?'

Mr Lewis was a wonderful painter, of the decorating variety, who was well into his seventies, but with a steady hand and a wonderful Cockney sense of humour. He probably had a Christian name, though to me he was always Mr Lewis. However much I told him that the opposite was true, he was convinced that my working life was an endless round of glamorous actresses auditioning for me, champagne parties 'up the 'Dilly' (as he quaintly called it) and a constant stream of international movie stars through the office. He made his first visit to 60 St James's Street to redecorate my office and, as space was limited, we shared the room, me on the telephone and him up a ladder. After he'd been at work for a couple of days, the door burst open and in walked a tall, blonde policewoman.

'You're under arrest,' she shouted, and Mr Lewis wobbled at the top of his ladder. 'For being the best agent in London!' At which point she stripped off down to her bra and fishnets, and sang me a song to the effect that

Peter Bowles was very grateful for the part we'd helped him get in 'To the Manor Born'. By this stage, Mr Lewis had given up painting and was sitting on his ladder in stunned silence. The girl disappeared to change and then returned to give me her card, plus a photo and CV.

'I'm really an actress,' she said. 'I just do this part time.'

'Of course you do,' I replied.

Later that week, Peter Bowles, resplendent in a cream overcoat, white fedora, co-respondent shoes and a red silk scarf, appeared in my office.

'Come to the window,' he said, 'I've something to show you.'

I looked down at the street and there was a white Rolls-Royce, gleaming in the St James's sunshine.

'Peter, thank you,' I said, 'I don't know what to say . . .'

'No, no,' spluttered Peter, 'it's mine. I've just bought it from Jack Barclay. You know my father was a Rolls-Royce chauffeur. Well, I always said that one day I'd own a Rolls and, thanks to you, I do. I wanted you to be the first person to see it.'

He sold it a year or so later because he kept getting recognized, perhaps because of the all-white ensemble of hat, coat and car.

As Mr Lewis was packing up his things a few days later, a famous actor came into the office to talk to Julian about some of our clients and a project he was involved with. He walked into my office.

'Hello, dear Michael,' he said.

'Larry, how lovely to see you. Oh, may I introduce Mr Lewis. Mr Lewis, do you know Sir Laurence Olivier?'

When I settled up with Mr Lewis, he said he never had believed that my life was a humdrum drudge of boring contracts and business telephone calls, as I'd pretended.

'I've had more excitement in the last week than I've had in my whole life.'

Sadly, he died the following year, not, I hope, as a result of all the activity in St James's Street.

Julian was a great lover of what he called 'a nightcap at the Bells'. This would entail a couple of hours at Annabel's over several kümmels, and then a drive home to his place off the New King's Road. One evening I left him as he took a brief detour via Shepherd Market and arrived home at 3 a.m. with a prostitute. His long-term girlfriend was away at the time. Avoiding the marital bed on ethical grounds, he remembered the girl taking off his trousers and then the heady mix of port and kümmel sent him into a deep sleep on the floor of the sitting room.

He woke up at 9 a.m. the next day in a state of some disarray. The girl had gone, as had his wallet, but everything else seemed to be OK. He had a bath and a shave, and then went into his bedroom. He opened the cupboard and pulled out a suit. It was as he reached the front door, and was about to leave the house, that he paused and thought back to having opened the cupboard.

Something had not been quite right. He went back to the bedroom, opened the long double cupboard again and shock, horror, all his girlfriend's clothes had vanished. She had been away overnight at a business meeting in Manchester and was due back at the house at 10 a.m. – he had twenty-five minutes. He rang his friend David Reoch, who was an insurance broker, and asked for his advice. David's business extended to insuring a few brothels in the West End, so Julian was candid with him.

'What you do, Julian, is this . . .' said David. 'Break a window and remove one or two small items – a radio, some silver or whatever. When your lady returns, tell her there was a break-in, and that all her clothes have been stolen. You've reported it to the police and rung me. I'll send you a claim form. Fill it in, return it to me, and I'll send you the money. Obviously I won't forward the claim on, so you'll have to reimburse me.'

'Fine,' said Julian.

His girlfriend returned home and, after a calming breakfast with Julian and a visit from Chelsea Glass, all seemed to be well. A couple of days later, they sat at the dining-room table and started to complete the claim form.

'Right,' said Julian, 'that leather jacket. What shall we say, a hundred pounds?'

'Oh no,' came the reply, 'it was much more than that. To replace it would cost at least five hundred.'

'N-no way,' spluttered Julian, 'it would never cost that. Let's say two hundred.'

'Why are you so worried about the price?' she said. 'We are insured, aren't we?'

'Of course,' lied Julian. 'So, how about three hundred?'

Having worked through the entire wardrobe at these kinds of prices, with Julian trying to lower them while his girlfriend constantly upped them, the final tally came to £3,500. David Reoch's cheque arrived a couple of weeks later, just as soon as Julian's one to him had cleared.

Over lunch at the Turf Club, Julian said, 'That was the most expensive fuck I've never had. The whole evening cost me well over four grand!'

I always had a sneaking suspicion that his girlfriend had guessed what had happened, or someone had told her, and she thought she'd better get her own back.

Julian's other great love was the 'green baize', as he called it. One evening, Julian and his friend Denis Milne asked me to join them for dinner at Casanova, an upmarket gaming club in Kensington, followed by a flutter or two at the tables. Denis seemed to be more interested in the dining part of the evening, given that it was all complimentary, and especially in what the sommelier was recommending. Flushed with the success of a good dinner with the added attraction of the 'big stamp', we went downstairs to the gaming area, where Denis spotted Robert Maxwell playing blackjack. Maxwell also seemed to be playing several other tables at the same time.

'How much are those chips he's putting on the roulette table?' I asked Julian.

'Five,' said Denis.

'Five pounds?' I asked.

'No, five hundred, and the bigger ones are a thousand,' said Julian.

'But he's not even looking at the roulette wheel. He doesn't seem to mind whether he wins or loses.'

'I'm going to have a word with him,' said Denis.

'Do you know him?' said Julian.

'No, of course not,' said Denis. 'But the man's supposed to be a bloody socialist. What's he doing gambling obscene amounts of money like that?'

'Maybe you shouldn't . . .' said Julian.

But it was too late. Denis had weaved his way over to where Maxwell was sitting and tapped him on the shoulder.

'Er, Mr Maxwell, might I ask you a question?' slurred Denis.

Silence.

'How do you . . . how can I put it . . . reconcile your socialist principles with . . .'

Silence.

'You are still a socialist, aren't you?'

Silence.

'How do you reconcile your socialist principles with gambling at a number of tables at once, some of which you can't even see?'

Silence.

'Frankly, I think it's wholly unacceptable, given . . .'

At which point Maxwell nodded to a dinner-jacketed goon, who was standing by the table. In a matter of seconds, Julian, Denis and I were being individually escorted down the hall towards the front door.

Julian's escort took his arm.

'Get your hands off me,' shouted Julian. 'Don't you know who I am?'

'Indeed, Mr Belfrage,' said the man. 'Out.'

And he was pushed gently out of the door into the crisp morning air of Gloucester Road.

'You'll be hearing more from me on this matter!' shouted Julian, as the heavy doors slammed in front of him.

'What about a nightcap somewhere?' said Denis.

In my early days at ICM, Robin Fox had invited me to a party at his flat in Eaton Square. It was littered with the *crème de la crème* – Dirk Bogarde, Paul Scofield, Laurence Olivier, Vanessa Redgrave, Robert Morley, Julie Christie, Alec Guinness and Albert Finney.

I sat on the sofa in star-struck awe, listening to Dirk talk to Julie about their latest film, as Robert Morley butted in with the odd theatrical anecdote. I joined in nervously with the roars of laughter. So this was the life of a top theatrical agent? I'll have some of this, I thought, as Robin's driver gave me a lift home in a sleek black

Mercedes. I remembered this moment five years later, shortly after we'd started Leading Artists.

Alan Stratford Johns, 'Charlie Barlow' of 'Z Cars', and I were having supper at San Lorenzo's in Wimbledon, after I'd seen him in a play. With several glasses of Sambucca aboard, I was ready for bed but Alan was ready to party.

'Let's go and have a nightcap with my son, Alan Junior; he lives just up the road.'

Reluctantly, I went with him to a grim-looking block of flats off Wimbledon High Street.

'It's very dark, Alan,' I said, 'and he's probably asleep.'

It was one o'clock in the morning. Alan rang the doorbell and then retreated into a nearby bush. 'I'm desperate for a slash,' he explained.

'Ring the doorbell again,' he shouted.

You didn't argue with Charlie Barlow.

The upstairs window opened, and an ashen face appeared. 'Who's that?'

'It's your Dad. I've got Michael with me. Can we come in for a beer?'

'Dad, I was asleep,' shouted Alan Junior. 'Why don't you just fuck off?'

'Charming,' said Alan, 'telling your father and his agent to fuck off. Just get down here and open the door.'

Alan Junior slammed the window shut and turned off all the lights.

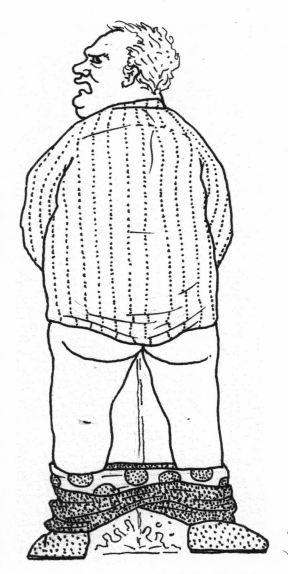

'You didn't argue with Charlie Barlow'

'To be honest, Alan, I wasn't that desperate for a beer, anyway,' I said helpfully.

'Rude little bugger,' Alan muttered as he stomped off up the road, leaving me to work out where I'd parked my car.

On the way home, I thought, 'This isn't what I wanted when I became an agent.' Where were Vanessa and Larry? Where was the gossip with Dirk and Julie? Where was the sleek black Mercedes? What was I doing south of the river? Whatever happened to Eaton Square? Was *this* the glamorous world of show business, I had aspired to? Surely not.

7

Private Lives

I met my first wife through a dating agency. Well, indirectly. People who use dating agencies always say they are doing it just for a bit of fun and I told my friends the same thing; but I was heading into my late twenties and wasn't exactly awash with girlfriends.

'You're not one of those, are you, dear?' asked Nora.

Maybe my years in the prep school business and an increasing interest in things theatrical had started to worry her.

'I do wish you'd find yourself a nice Catholic girl,' she said. 'What about that Anne Porter? She's such a nice girl, and her father is a doctor, you know.'

Nora was clearly blinded by that Porter girl's niceness and her doctor father, but had missed the fact that she was one of the most unattractive girls I had ever met. She had a rasping high-pitched squeak of a voice and smelt of cats. Nora had always held the Porters in high esteem ever since Dr Porter had given her a pair of tickets to the

Royal Academy Summer Exhibition Private View, which he'd been given by a grateful patient.

'Jack would never have got me tickets for the Royal Academy,' she said. 'The last time he came home with tickets was when the fur buyer at Gorringes gave him two for the Motor Show.'

There were girls, naturally, and I had had several reasonably steady relationships but nothing special. So I signed on to Computerdate, which offered its subscribers the names of three supposedly compatible partners in return for a handsome fee. Having completed the form, I thought I sounded like a bit of a catch: tall, dark, blue-eyed, a good sense of humour (would anyone ever admit to having *no* sense of humour?), a lover of pop and classical music, who enjoyed going to parties, the theatre, the cinema, restaurants and concerts.

The following week I was sent a card, on which three names and telephone numbers were printed. That evening I called Lady Number One. The voice was husky, sexy and foreign; she was Swiss and presumably lonely. We made a date for later that week at a restaurant off Kensington High Street. She was very tall, much taller than me, blonde and rather good-looking. Unfortunately that was about as far as it went: she spoke little English and talked incessantly about her parents in Zürich; her father had something to do with refrigeration. I made a mental note not to commit to more than a drink with ladies two and three. I probably bundled her out of the restaurant rather too quickly and suggested lamely that we keep in touch.

Lady Number Two was an altogether different proposition, on the telephone at least: seductive voice, good sense of humour and keen to meet for a drink, which we did the following evening. Now I've got nothing against spots per se, and indeed, as a young man, I was plagued from time to time by bouts of eczema (Ampleforth was a hotbed of skin allergies in the 1950s), but Lady Number Two had virtually no facial surface that wasn't affected by a spot, cyst or blister. Her face was an eruption of livid, peeling skin. Of course I felt sorry for her, but was this the girl of my dreams? As far as I was concerned, my love on this occasion was skin-deep. Conversation ran out of steam so quickly that, on hearing her family lived near Brighton, I found myself talking to her about the train service from Victoria and asking whether she ever drove to Brighton. ('Erm . . . do you take the A3, or cut through Wimbledon on the A23?') Desperate stuff.

Despite my having decided not to pursue Lady Number Three, curiosity got the better of me a few weeks later.

'I'm off to Australia in a couple of days; I was expecting you to call ages ago,' she said.

'I've been in New York,' I lied.

'Do you want to meet this evening?' she asked.

I agreed to go to her flat in Fulham, opposite Chelsea football ground, which she was moving out of, and which she shared with two other girls.

Unfortunately, Lady Number Three was short, dumpy, hearty and never stopped talking, mainly about skiing. I've never quite seen the point of skiing, and she certainly put me off it for life. Her flatmates were sweet: one spent most of the time I was there talking to her mother on the telephone; the other had a drippy boyfriend attached to her hand while she cooked supper. After the obligatory promises of keeping in touch, I headed for the front door. There was a lot of activity in the hall and in staggered an extremely pretty girl in a huge purple hat, carrying an array of boxes, bags and cases. Lady Number Three introduced me to her; she was taking over her room in the flat. I helped her with her luggage and, after a brief chat, discovered where she worked. I called her the following morning, though by then I had forgotten her name.

An attractive voice answered the telephone.

'May I speak to the girl with the purple hat?' I mumbled.

'Speaking,' she replied.

We were married a year later.

Jane and I were very good friends but, unfortunately, the friendship lasted longer than the marriage. She was in her early twenties and trying to get a career going working for Laurence Olivier at the Old Vic. We parted five years later in a reasonably amicable way, and Jane went on marry Tim Rice.

★　★　★

I was reluctantly on the dating scene again – well, perhaps not *that* reluctantly. I had a fairly hot and heavy relationship with Lynne Frederick, whom I represented, thereby totally disregarding Laurie's earlier advice. Lynne went on to marry David Frost and then Peter Sellers. Sadly her life ratcheted out of control after Seller's death, and she died in her late thirties. She was certainly the marrying kind, but I didn't feel ready for another trip up the aisle so soon after my last one.

Maria Aitken's mother, Pempe, invited me to her house in Phillimore Gardens, where I met Margaret Thatcher's daughter. Carol had been going out with Maria's brother, Jonathan, but that relationship had come to a sudden end; and Pempe was trying to do a spot of match-making.

Carol and I went out together over a period of a few months – she was great fun to be with – and I then found myself being ushered up the stairs of No. 10 Downing Street to meet 'Mum and Dad'.

The Thatchers were very warm and friendly, and after too many scotches in their cosy flat at the top of the house it was time to head home. I went into the hall with Carol to ring for a cab.

'Pick–up address, guv?' said the voice at the end of the telephone.

'No. 10 Downing Street,' I replied.

'Oh yes, and your name?'

'Whitehall,' I said, unfortunately followed by a slightly slurred giggle.

'Most amusing, sir.'

'N-no, really,' I started, as Carol grabbed the phone, neither slurry nor giggling.

'Have you got that?' she asked.

'Yes,' replied the voice, 'I've got a cab for a Mr Whitehall who wants to be picked up from 10 Downing Street. And what would your name be, madam?' he enquired.

'Thatcher,' she replied sternly. The telephone went dead.

I picked up a cab in Whitehall.

And then, like a hurricane, Victoria came into my life. I had met her at a party in the mid-1970s, and we had lived together, on and off, until 1984 – probably more off than on. She was away a lot, often for three or more months at a time, crewing on boats (not a love I shared with her, being unable to swim and prone to seasickness) or just travelling around the world at my expense – to France, Italy, Antigua, Corsica, Sardinia – while I stayed at home in Barnes and waited for sporadic phone calls. Finally, she sent me a 'Dear John' letter from Sardinia, having been there for five months. 'All I can say,' she wrote, 'is sorry.'

By then I was relieved: the relationship had been a mistake from the start. When Victoria finally returned to London, she came to see me. (By that time I was living in Hammersmith.) I gave her some money and she moved out. Well, there wasn't much to move out because, despite living with me for eight years or so, she had never really moved in. The portrait of her grand-father by Percy Wyndham Lewis, which I greatly coveted, went as did the packed suitcase in the spare room for what she called 'a quick getaway'. She did, however, return a month or so later when I was on holiday in Greece and took away a vanload of furniture which she claimed was hers. And that was that, until two years later, one Saturday morning, the postman called.

A firm of City solicitors, representing Victoria, were writing to inform me that she was looking for a half-share in my house and business. So not much then. The letter asked me for my financial proposals; though the only proposal I could immediately think of was that Victoria should get lost. Nevertheless, I thought I'd better get a second opinion. I telephoned Philip Havers, Nigel's barrister brother, and read him the letter.

'Why don't you call Dad?' he suggested.

Dad was Sir Michael Havers, Attorney General, soon to be Lord Chancellor: rather heavyweight, I thought, to be advising me on an errant girlfriend, particularly on Saturday morning.

'Dad won't mind,' said Philip. 'He'd be annoyed if you didn't.'

'Let's have lunch next week,' said Sir Michael. 'I'll meet you at the Berkeley at one o'clock next Tuesday.'

When Havers arrived with two other men, I began to worry that I was out of my depth.

'John, Graham, Michael Whitehall,' said Havers.

'Good afternoon, sir,' they said and sat down at the next table.

'Bodyguards,' explained Havers.

'She's certainly not getting any more money out of me,' I said. 'I've been bankrolling her for years. She can go fuck herself.'

He agreed up to a point but, having read the letter over a couple of times, he surprised me by saying, 'The only thing about this letter that worries me is the last paragraph.'

'Which bit?' I asked.

'The bit that says, "Our client is legally aided."'

Somehow Victoria had managed to make the legal aid board believe her hard–luck story and secure the services of a solicitor and barrister.

'So, I don't think telling her "to go fuck herself" will quite solve the problem,' said Havers. 'Well, certainly not at this stage anyway. If I were you I'd get yourself a decent divorce lawyer. I'll suggest a couple,' he said.

'Now, what would you like to start with?' asked Sir Michael. 'The smoked salmon's very good here.'

The Chancery Division of the High Court, 1 May 1989. Stephen Miller, a colleague of Philip Havers, presented his case to Mr Justice Millett, a tall, balding member of the celebrated outdoor clothing and equipment dynasty (and probably not a judge with an encyclopaedic knowledge of actors). No mistaking Victoria's man, David

'Probably not a judge with an encyclopaedic knowledge of actors'

Schmitz: too much hair under his wig, big glasses, stubbly, a man with the look of legal aid about him.

'A bit of a rights-for-women type,' said Stephen.

I was jolly pleased, however, to have the cool, sleek Miller on my side, and not the stubbly Schmitz.

After both barristers made their opening speeches, Millett asked them to approach the bench, where he told Schmitz that his initial response to the submissions was unfavourable – he could see little for him to find for the plaintiff on what he had heard so far. Schmitz assured him that there was a lot more to come – which, as it transpired, there really wasn't.

During the lunch break, over a relaxing pee in the barristers' lavatories, Messrs Miller and Schmitz discussed the morning's events. Stephen thought it might be a good moment for Mr Schmitz to heed the judge's words. It was fine for his client, who was on legal aid, but Stephen's wasn't. More importantly, a case lasting two weeks, which this one could easily stretch to, might cost his client £100,000 or more, win or lose. Surely the thing to do would be to call it a day now. (I believe this was the gist of their conversation; I wasn't actually in the loo with them.) Schmitz would have none of it. He clearly thought that by winning the case – the first 'palimony' case in England and Wales – he could have the law amended. Quite a challenge.

Stephen explained to me over a sandwich that it was difficult for the judge to do any more than advise at this early stage. If he presented his views too strongly, Schmitz could have grounds for a retrial, or at least an appeal, which would incur even more costs.

'But I'm sure we'll win,' said Stephen. 'Well, pretty sure anyway; unless Schmitz has something nasty up his sleeve.'

Victoria's schmoozing had obviously worked on Mr Schmitz. All he appeared to have up his sleeve was a list of increasingly bizarre questions. He seemed to have no idea how my business worked or what I actually did for a living, and he had a wholly random take on Victoria. Her wronged-little-woman role failed to convince everyone in court except him.

'Is it true that Victoria sat up all night with Edward Fox, discussing his career?' enquired Schmitz.

'No,' I replied.

'Did Jeffrey Archer seek advice about his latest book from Victoria in your bedroom?'

'No.'

'At a time when Victoria was suffering from severe influenza?'

'No.'

'Did Victoria arrange champagne parties for your clients three times a week?'

'No.'

On the first day of the case the press gallery was empty, but as soon as Victoria got into the witness box, dropping names like confetti, it started to fill up. Unfortunately, the papers were full of ghastly headlines, thanks to this penchant of Victoria's. 'TV AGENT IN LOVENEST BATTLE', 'I WANT MY SHARE SAYS MISTRESS' and 'I HELPED SAVE YOUR BUSINESS, EX-LOVER TELLS SHOWBIZ AGENT' were some of the more lurid headlines.

Victoria was always referred to as my mistress although, of course, she wasn't, since I was unmarried, but it gave the headlines a bit of extra spice. A favourite was: 'MY ALL-STAR PARTIES FOR LOVER WHO SPURNED ME'. Very classy stuff.

One of Victoria's stranger witnesses was a producer acquaintance of mine with whom I'd fallen out over a deal, and who subsequently spent some time at Her Majesty's pleasure in HMP Ford. Dressed in a mauve hound's-tooth check suit, with the look of a bookie's runner about him, he started to give his evidence to a perplexed Mr Justice Millett. He told Millett, in far too chummy a fashion, what a remarkable woman Victoria was, and how lucky I had been to meet her. Mature and confident, she had pulled me up by my bootlaces and introduced me to a world I had only ever dreamed of – a world of fine art, literature, vintage wine and elegant living. He paused, and I waited for him to tell Schmitz what he thought of me.

'This is where the knife goes in,' whispered Stephen.

'And tell us about Mr Whitehall?' asked Schmitz.

'Michael is a great guy. Charming, talented and a

wonderful friend, as well as an astute businessman who I admire enormously.'

'This chap's not going to be any use to anyone,' Stephen continued. 'He doesn't want to upset either of you. Useless witness. There's no point in cross-examining him. And where the hell did he get that suit from?'

During the final few days of the trial, a tall middle-aged woman in a uniform arrived in the court with Victoria.

'Who's the *Gruppenführer*, sitting next to Victoria?' Stephen asked.

'It's Victoria's mother. She used to be in the WRVS and seems to have got the uniform out of mothballs to impress Millett.'

He looked unimpressed, despite her persistence in grinning at him.

During his summing up, Mr Justice Millett said, referring to one of Victoria's earlier trips abroad, 'In July, when she reached Djibouti, she found waiting for her a telegram from Mr Whitehall and a return ticket to London. She flew home. On her arrival, she was handed a passionate letter from Mr Whitehall, which did not deserve the fate of being photocopied by lawyers four-teen years later, and included in the agreed bundle for the use of the court.'

Shit, I thought, I can see tomorrow's headlines now: 'TV AGENT'S PASSIONATE LETTER TO CHAMPAGNE MISTRESS FOUND IN AGREED BUNDLE'.

It was a great relief to hear Mr Justice Millett say, 'I dismiss the action', and the following morning to read, 'PALIMONY CASE BLONDE SENT PACKING WITHOUT A PENNY'.

For someone who had hitherto successfully kept himself out of the papers, this was all quite a shock. When Elaine Stritch came back from New York at the end of the case, she rang me. 'Darling, I'm back in London, and you're all over the papers. You've become a celebrity. I'm worried. It's *me* I want all over the papers, not *you*!' I'd never come close to the cult of celebrity before and I didn't enjoy my five minutes of fame a bit. When I went back to work, feeling rather sad about the whole pointless affair, Julian popped his head around my office door. 'I always thought Victoria was a bloody nuisance,' he said, 'but I didn't like to tell you.'

One Sunday morning I had a call from Maria Aitken.

'I'm having a party, and would love you to come,' she said.

'That would be great. When is it?'

'Tonight, actually. Eight-ish at the flat?'

'How nice of you to think of me, Maria.'

'I know it sounds a bit last minute, but we put the whole thing together very late.'

When I arrived at the flat, the place was heaving. How clever of Maria, I thought, to get so many grand people together at such short notice – even the Pinters were there. Maria released me from the clutches of Jill Bennett and introduced me to a couple standing by the buffet table.

'Hilary and Earl, this is Michael Whitehall.'

Earl was a smart, middle-aged American with suspiciously dark black hair; Hilary was a very attractive brunette in her early twenties with big green eyes. I was smitten.

'Hilary is my understudy in the play,' explained Maria.

But, who was Earl, I wondered? Were they married or just an item? He looked very camp, not at all the marrying kind, but so did I in my white suit and pink tie. I caught up with Hilary later.

'How long have you and Earl been together?' I asked.

'Oh, I only met him when he offered to help me at the buffet table,' said Hilary. 'I think he's some actor's boyfriend.'

Hilary explained that she'd been rung by Maria that afternoon and asked to come because they were short of girls. Perhaps they were short of men too, I thought. I discovered that Hilary had been an actress since leaving school, but didn't have an agent. She gave me her telephone number.

'I'll call and fix up a date for you to come and see me. I wouldn't be able to take you on myself,' I said rather grandly, 'but I could give you a few names and a bit of advice.'

Hilary looked impressed – I certainly was.

...an Le Mesurier, a.k.a. Daphne du Maurier

'I'm most certainly *not* gay, madam.'
Dinsdale Landen and dog

Sinking fast in the Peloponnese

With Nigel Havers and Julian Fellowes
on the set of *Lord Elgin*

Hilary's parents reserving judgement in Winchester

artin Jarvis and Edward Fox provide an umbrella escort at Hammersmith egister Office

Bride, groom and usher, Moray Watson,
await the arrival of the best man

Confettied by Judi Dench

Being seen with me was better for his image than a new bimbo every night

f only . . .

aniel Day-Lewis's first footing at 125 Gloucester Road

Nigel Havers on location bonding with his godson Jack

Celebrity party-time at Bob Monkhouse's; Elaine Stritch in a summer hat

With Peter Bowles in his
country casuals

Withnail and I

Travelling players on the *QE2* between infusions of Beluga caviar

Richard Griffiths and the Whitehalls on Broadway

The following day I left a message on her answering machine to call me, and then headed off to Ireland to see Peter Bowles and John Wells, who were filming *The Irish RM* for ITV. While I was there I tried her again, and left another message. On my return to the office, a few days later, she hadn't rung back and I decided to put her out of my mind. She wasn't that exciting anyway and far too young for me. Ten days later, Amanda Fitzalan-Howard, my long-suffering assistant, rang through to say that Hilary was on the line.

'Tell her I'm in a meeting,' I said grumpily.

She rang again later.

'I'll call her back,' I said.

Amanda came into my office. 'Hilary's rung four times now. She seems really nice. Why won't you speak to her?'

'Look, Amanda,' I replied, 'I rang her twice after we met at Maria's, and she couldn't even be bothered to ring me back. That was nearly two weeks ago. It's too late now. Bloody actresses.'

'She's been in the States.'

'What?'

'She left the day after Maria's party.'

'Hilary, how are you?' I said. 'Sorry, but we seem to keep missing each other.'

She explained that she'd been to the States for a fortnight to sort out her private life. Could she come and see me?

'Certainly,' I said, 'how about tomorrow morning?'

Sitting on the sofa in my office, Hilary looked even younger and more delectable than she had in Maria's flat. As I was flannelling her about choosing the right agent — which, of course, was one of the most important decisions in an actress's life, there being so many sharks out there and most agents being interested in only one thing — my door burst open and in walked Judi Dench.

'You dirty old man, Michael,' said Judi, as she saw Hilary, in a short skirt, sitting on my sofa. I introduced Hilary to Judi, and after some small talk Judi left to talk to Julian.

Hilary was clearly *very* impressed.

Not only was Michael a big player in the theatrical world, he was joshing with one of her great idols. Hilary then told me that she was about to do a play in Northampton. Would I come and see her?

'Unfortunately, I don't do up north,' I said, 'but I'll try and send someone from the office.' (I hadn't realized that Northampton wasn't that far north.)

I walked her to Piccadilly Circus tube. Although I was free for lunch, and she looked as though she was too, I thought I might look like one of those agents I'd warned her against, so resisted the temptation.

After going out for a couple of months, it was time for me to be introduced to Hilary's parents. All they knew about me was that I was 'older' than Hilary and that I was a theatrical agent, neither of which was a great plus from their point of view. We decided to meet on neutral ground: lunch at their son's town house in Winchester which had previously been owned by a wheelchair-bound writer. I had a problem squeezing the Jaguar XJS into a very narrow space outside the house. Much roaring and revving caught the attention of Hilary's mother.

'Don't hit my car,' she shouted.

'Please be careful,' said Hilary, 'they've only just bought it.'

Lunch went reasonably well and I tried to keep the conversation light. My arrival in the Jaguar had clearly created the wrong impression (Hilary's mother thought it looked rather flash) and the two-pound box of Godiva chocolates for her was clearly a mistake ('I can't be bought'). Hilary's father was clearly shocked by my age: I wasn't much younger than he was. A rather complicated and ultimately unfunny anecdote, involving an Anderson Shelter in the Blitz, got the post–luncheon walk off to a bad start.

As it was getting dark, we made our exit and headed off to the car. Hilary's family waved from the window as I shuffled down the steps, trying to get my footing while waving at the window.

'It's a wrap,' shouted Hilary from the car, a show business term loosely meaning a job done. Still shuffling, I smiled back at her and back up at the window.

'It's a . . .'

I cupped my ears to hear what she was saying. It wasn't 'It's a wrap'; it was 'It's a ramp.'

The previous owner had put a ramp over the front steps to accommodate his wheelchair, hence my shuffle.

I got into the XJS, knocking Hilary's mother's wing mirror in the process, and gingerly backed out the car. As we drove off I could feel several pairs of eyes boring into the back of my greying head.

'I'm reserving judgment,' said Hilary's mother when Hilary telephoned her on our return. 'Bill thought he was older than he'd expected. How old is he?'

'I don't know exactly, Mummy, mid-forties, I think.'

'But you're only twenty-two, darling. He's far too old for you,' she said. 'And Bill wasn't sure about that car. He's worried he might just be after one thing. You know what they say about agents.'

Hilary later told me that when we had first met at Maria's flat, she'd thought that Earl was probably more my type.

A few months later, Hilary and I headed off to Greece to visit Nigel Havers, who was making a film for Channel 4. Christopher Miles thought a film about Lord Elgin *had* to be made. I'm always suspicious of a film that 'has to be made': it presupposes that the subject matter is begging to be put on the screen, when in reality it is the producer, director or writer who is doing the begging, in this case one and the same person. 'The nation has a right to see "Never the Twain" at Christmas,' the director Anthony Parker once told me when ITV cancelled a

Christmas special of the less than perfect comedy series, starring my client Donald Sinden. Or was it Mr Parker who thought he had a right to direct it?

Nevertheless, Christopher, brother of the actress Sarah Miles, had managed to get Channel 4 to put up the money for a TV film. Nigel Havers was to play Elgin, with support from Hugh Grant, Julian Fellowes and Clare Byam-Shaw, and the film was to be shot on location in and around a one-horse town called Methoni, on the west coast of the Peloponnese. Prior to a short holiday in Corfu, I decided to make a location visit with Hilary.

Nigel met us at Kalamata Airport late in the afternoon, and by the time we arrived at Methoni it was pitch dark. However, before taking us to our beach hotel − which was plunged into darkness by a power cut, just as we arrived − Nigel wanted to show us the sights. Clearly happy to see us, he roared up and down the long beach in his hire car, thinking it might be fun to skim the edge of the water to create a big splash. After a few dramatic cascades he misjudged the angle of approach and drove straight into the sea. The car ground to a halt in the sand and water started to pour through the bottom of the doors.

'This place is the most terrible dump, but they're very sweet. I'll see if I can raise someone,' said Nigel.

Parked up the beach by the hotel was a campervan which had a flickering light coming from within. Although it was by now almost midnight, Nigel ran up the beach and banged on the window. A large German appeared.

'I know it's late and I'm most awfully sorry to disturb you, but my car has got stuck in the sand. It's a hire car actually, so I'm quite keen not to lose it. Do you by any chance have a towrope? The car is floating just down there.'

Meanwhile Hilary was enjoying her first location visit with her successful agent boyfriend by lugging our bags up the beach in the dark; her dress was hitched up, and she was covered in seawater and sand. I managed to keep cameras, videos and assorted Dunhill accessories out of the water. After what seemed like hours, we assembled a pile of tawdry-looking bags outside the hotel, which seemed to have been locked up for the night.

Nigel and the German were on their way down the beach to inspect the hire car. The German explained that, while he was happy to try and pull the car out of the sand, his wife and child were asleep in the campervan, so he didn't want us to make too much noise. Having managed to secure a towrope from under his wife's sleeping body, he drove the campervan down the beach. He attached the rope to the front of the car, which now had water flowing through it pretty freely, and started up his van. After several unsuccessful attempts to pull the car out, the campervan got stuck. The more the German revved, the deeper the campervan sank into the sand. By now the German's wife and child were awake, and Nigel had to carry them up the beach and deposit them on our luggage. As he came back, he saw that the campervan had sunk deeper than the hire car. No wonder the German's demeanour took a turn for the worse, and he started ranting at us in a way that only a German can.

By now someone had stirred in the hotel. The owner, a Zorba look-alike, with no English and certainly no German, suggested in sign language that we contact a farmer on the other side of town, who, for a price, would pull both vehicles out of the sea with his tractor. The German helpfully pointed out that seawater was not good for the interior of motor vehicles, especially their engines.

Zorba and Nigel headed off to the farm and returned twenty minutes later on a tractor, accompanied by a surly-looking farmer. It was now one o'clock in the morning, and the farmer hadn't taken Nigel's request for help well; though his mood did change when a not inconsiderable number of drachmas changed hands. The tractor pulled out the German with some difficulty, but Nigel's car popped out of the sea with ease and the farmer deposited it on the road at the top of the beach. The car was a sorry sight: the water had reached the level of the steering wheel, and a rather elegant linen jacket I'd brought especially for the Methoni trip was floating forlornly above the back seat.

The following day we met the rest of the cast. Hugh Grant had missed the events of the previous night, as he'd been out until morning at a mystery location, apparently a fairly regular pattern of his time in Greece. He confided in Hilary later that he had a penchant for dirty girls; Hilary was loath to pry further in case he thought she might be interested in joining the harem. Julian Fellowes was the life and soul of the party, and Clare Byam-Shaw had that far-away look in her eye, suggesting that Nigel's attentions may not have been entirely focused on his script during his time in the Peloponnese.

When we returned home from Corfu, the crew had moved on to Athens, though I'd heard from Christopher Miles that Nigel's hire car had been abandoned in Methoni. Late one evening we telephoned Nigel at his hotel. Hilary's father, who was staying with us, pretended to be 'Hugh Beesley' from the night desk in the Greek section of the Foreign Office. Unfortunately we miscalculated the time difference, ringing Nigel at 2 a.m. rather than what we thought was 11 p.m. A bleary voice answered the phone.

'Mr Havers? Hugh Beesley here, from the Foreign Office. We've had a complaint from our Greek friends about a wrecked car, hired out to you, which has been found on Methoni beach. As you know, the political situation in Greece is very fragile at the moment, and we're worried that this could cause a major diplomatic incident.'

Nigel sounded bleary and concerned.

'What are your proposals with regard to this matter?' At which point I giggled.

Nigel, quick as a flash, replied, 'My proposals are that it is two o'clock in the morning, and you can tell Michael Whitehall to go and fuck himself.'

For our honeymoon Hilary was looking for something hot, sunny and relaxing, and far away from any showbiz types. The travel brochures all pointed in the direction of the Seychelles.

On arrival at Mahé, after a grim nine-hour flight, we were greeted by a coach, listing the six hotels to which it was going. The Sunset Beach Hotel was the last on the list: it was going to be a long trip with forty people jammed into a small bus.

'Still worth it, though,' I said cheerily. 'Just look at this place – it's paradise. It's true what they say: if you want it hot and unspoilt, you have to travel. And actually that nine-hour flight wasn't too bad.'

'It's amazingly lush,' replied Hilary. This had already occurred to me.

'Not unlike England, apart from the palm trees,' I mused, looking out of the window. At which point I heard a whizzing sound, something I would hear a lot of over the coming fortnight. The coach driver had switched on his windscreen wipers. It poured with rain for the rest of the day.

On the bright side, the hotels at which we first stopped looked promising. By the time we arrived at the Sunset Beach, we were down to six passengers, and everything outside was starting to look soggy. This hotel was not in the same league as the others; its appearance was certainly not helped by a power cut, a consequence of the storms of the previous night. The candlelight may have been romantic but not entirely practical when trying to unpack. Our room had also been flooded, so we were moved to a room the size of a dormitory.

'This will just be for one night,' said the harassed-looking receptionist. 'It's a large family room so there are six single beds. But your room, one of four honeymoon suites, will be ready in the morning.'

In fact it never was; we spent a lot of time in the dormitory. We had an ongoing wet-weather programme of badminton, and the hotel television had a selection of British TV hits, including 'The Sweeney' and 'The Gentle Touch', on a loop. The six single beds pushed together gave us a spacious, if rather lumpy, king-sized double bed, ideal for a newly married couple.

As we sat in the bar drinking, we were approached by a large man in Bermuda shorts and a T-shirt.

'Your first trip here?' he asked in a loud American drawl.

'Yes, actually. Shame about the weather,' I said.

'It's like this most of the time,' said his wife, also large and in shorts. 'When we arrived we thought all the umbrellas were to keep the sun off. Boy were we wrong!'

They bought us a drink, and in an attempt to get off the weather I brightly asked them where they lived.

'New York City. Do you know New York?'

'Yes, a bit.'

'And what do you do?'

'Jed's in the motion picture business,' interrupted his wife.

We made our excuses and retired to our 'honeymoon' dormitory.

The following morning the rain had eased off and we headed for the beach. Thick grey clouds disappeared, to reveal a clear blue sky and blazing hot sun — far too hot for me. Hilary sunbathed while I sat in a beachside café reading. It was there that I met Serge.

'You like to snorkel?' he asked.

'No, thank you,' I replied, returning to my book.

'I take you snorkelling in the bay.'

I didn't want to get into a lot of detail with this young Seychellois, like telling him I couldn't actually swim. Fortunately, Hilary came up from the beach and took over. They had a long conversation about rocks, fish and snorkelling, and Hilary said she'd catch up with him later in the holiday.

We saw rather a lot of Serge after that. He was good company, full of local gossip, and amusing. We also saw a lot of our fellow guests at the Sunset Beach. One couple in particular became very attached to us. Allan and Joan Parker were also on their honeymoon, but clearly on their second or third marriages. They lived in a bungalow in Wisbech, where Allan had been a bus driver, having recently lost his job; Joan worked in a supermarket in

Lowestoft. Allan was a heavy smoker, hated the sun (in the Seychelles he seemed to have found his perfect holiday destination) and had little conversation apart from caravaning, in which he and Joan indulged on a regular basis. Allan also had a fondness for the local tropical punch and, when in his cups, would regale Hilary with stories of broken-down buses on the A216 and camping holidays from hell. Needless to say, avoiding the Parkers became one of our honeymoon's main challenges. Catching an hour on the beach in between heavy showers, Serge invited us to go snorkelling with him later that afternoon. Hilary explained that I was not a 'strong' swimmer, but that she would be delighted to join him for a swim around the bay. At the appointed time, I waved them off from the beach and returned to my dormitory for an afternoon snooze.

'Do you think I'll be all right with Serge?'

I woke up to find Hilary changing.

'I'm going to put on a T-shirt under my swimming costume: it might well be cold out there. So, do you think it's OK?'

I assured Hilary that it all would be fine: Serge seemed a really nice chap and apparently he'd been around the hotel for years.

'OK, if you think so. I'm meeting him in ten minutes and will be back in an hour or so. See you later.'

Hilary left the room, and I dozed off, reading my complimentary copy of *Seychelles Living*. When I woke up, it was starting to get dark but there was no sign of Hilary. I checked my watch — six o'clock — two hours since she'd left; she was probably having a drink with Serge. Nice chap. Suddenly the door burst open and there she was, standing in the doorway, cold, wet, dishevelled and bleeding.

'Thank God I put that T-shirt on under my bathing costume,' she said, as she sat down on the bed. She then told me all.

Having snorkelled around for half an hour or so, the water had become choppy, so they decided to swim to the shore of a small cove. Unable to find any sand, she had hitched herself up on to the top of a jagged rock, only to cut herself in the process. Serge lifted himself out of the water and joined her. He then proceeded to pull down the straps of her bathing costume in one experienced, double-handed movement.

'Hilaria, my love, I sex your body now,' he announced.

'Hilaria' was definitely not looking for sex; a towel or a plaster for her cut leg maybe, but not sex and certainly not sex with Serge.

'Serge, *please*,' she said, 'I'm on my honeymoon.'

'I have many honeymoon girls,' said Serge, hoping to reassure her.

'Michael would kill you,' she said.

'Michael, he is your father?'

'No, he's my husband, Serge. We've just got married.'

Serge, clearly sensing that this particular body sexing was going to require more groundwork than usual, took a different tack. 'But he is too old for you. He is like your father. You should have younger man – like me.'

Hilary wasn't at this point looking for marriage guidance counselling, but decided, with her bathing costume being the only protection between her and Serge's manhood, to change the conversation.

'Were you born in Mahé?'

They then had a chat about Serge's life, his parents, his siblings and his hopes for the future.

'One day I plan to go to America and work on boats,' he said. 'I like American girls: they are always very friendly.'

Sensing Serge might have been heading back in the direction of body sexing, Hilary jumped off the rock on to the narrow beach.

'I must get back to the hotel. Michael will be worrying about me.' She headed up the grassy bank in the direction of the hotel, pleased to discover, on looking back, that Serge was still sitting on the rock pensively, presumably having lost his primal urges after his long chat.

'I'll kill that fucker,' I said, leaping to my feet. 'Bloody little shit. Where is he?'

Now Serge was clearly a fucker, and indeed a shit, but he certainly wasn't little. He had the look of a young Johnny Weissmuller about him, and I would undoubtedly have been the loser in any beach-based altercation.

'Let's just forget it, Michael,' said Hilary.

That evening Serge appeared at the bar with some friends.

'Right, I'm going to sort him,' I said, pulling up my Bermuda shorts.

'Please, Michael, just leave it alone. *Please.*'

So I did, in a cowardly way.

Our last evening, like our first, involved an overly long conversation with the Americans.

'So, you're in the motion picture business?' I asked. 'Where are you based?'

'New York City,' he replied.

'And what particular branch of the movie business are you in?'

'Motion picture hardware.'

'Which is?'

'Cameras, tripods, lenses . . .'

'And what do you do with them?'

'We rent them out. Give me a call when you're in New York.'

Motion pictures indeed.

As our plane took off from Mahé Airport, we saw another plane land. No doubt a few young honeymooners would soon sample the pleasures of an afternoon's snorkelling with Serge. When we got home there was a postcard from the Parkers, hoping we'd had as good a time as they'd had.

8

Financial Affairs

For the most part, actors resent paying agents' commission. They don't mind paying their accountant or their doctor, but they do mind paying their agent. Or, indeed, paying for anything else involving agents. 'Can the agency pay for this?' says the actor to the agent, conveniently forgetting that the agency will be paying the restaurant bill from its 10 per cent, rather than from the actor's 90 per cent. Over the years, I have come across many restaurant bills that curled up on the table until I finally picked them up. Many actors accept commission as a part of life, but a few will go to any lengths to avoid it.

One such was Leslie Phillips. I had known Leslie for many years and thought that he was brilliant at what he did, but I was never convinced that he possessed quite the range he thought he had. I was always suspicious of using comic actors in serious parts – was it rather gimmicky? I looked after Jimmy Jewel, of Jewel & Warris fame, after he'd had a great success at the National in Trevor Griffiths's play *Comedians*. Jimmy then thought he was a proper actor, but I was never so sure. I think the problem using comics in so-called 'straight' parts is that the persona of the comic is usually stronger than that of the character he's playing. Norman Wisdom, Bob Monkhouse or Russ Abbott going 'legit' never quite works for me.

Leslie Phillips wanted to put his *Carry On* image behind him; no more lecherous dentists or randy car salesmen for him: he wanted to go to the National Theatre or the RSC and do some proper acting. Julian and I said we'd give it a try. And we did. We tried and tried and tried, and finally we got an offer for him to join the National. Leslie was very excited at the prospect until I told him what the money was.

'I couldn't possibly do it for that,' he said. 'Go back and get some more.'

I explained that the money was their 'special top'; not just their 'top' but their '*special* top' − topper than top. Gielgud money. McKellen money. Dench money.

'Well I'm sorry, I couldn't possibly do it for that.'

So Leslie didn't go to the National, or the RSC, or anywhere else. But he did make it clear to Julian and me that he was looking to move his career in a different direction. He'd even shave off his moustache if necessary.

A few weeks later, the theatrical producer, John Gale, sent me a new play by Michael Pertwee called *Sextet*. The plot centred on yachts, ex-wives, mistresses, philandering and general marital mayhem. John was very keen for me to send the play to Leslie. I explained that Leslie's career was moving in a different direction, and that playing a randy, philandering yachtsman was not it. But I promised to pass the play on to him, without holding out any hope that he would be interested.

Leslie was upset. How could I have sent him a play about a randy, philandering sailor? I knew that he wanted to move his career in other directions – Anouilh, Brecht, Chekhov, Molière, Pinter, Rattigan and Stoppard. These were the kind of writers with whom he wanted to be associated, not Michael Pertwee. He was annoyed and hurt that I had completely ignored his instructions; so hurt, in fact, that he saw no point in continuing our professional relationship. He was leaving me. 'No great loss,' said Julian. 'I thought the play was terrible. Imagine if he'd wanted to do it; we'd have had to sit through the bloody first night and buy him dinner afterwards. A blessing in disguise.'

I wrote Leslie a charming letter, expressing my regret and disappointment, wishing him luck for the future and asking him to let me know when he was fixed up with a new agent so that I could forward his post. And I let John Gale know that Leslie, as I had suspected, wasn't interested in *Sextet*.

A few weeks later, I had another telephone call from John. Would Dinsdale Landen be available for *Sextet*? I said that he was technically free, but wasn't he a touch on the young side for the raunchy old seadog?

'It's not for *that* part,' said John, 'it's for the friend.'

'He certainly wouldn't be interested in playing the friend,' I replied. Nobody's ever interested in playing the friend. 'But I'm sure he'd read the other part.'

'That's cast, I'm afraid.'

'Who with?'

'Leslie Phillips.'

John explained that he had been surprised when Leslie had telephoned him direct. Leslie had told him that I was no longer his agent, and that he had decided not to engage a new agent for the time being. Nevertheless, he would like another look at *Sextet*.

'I did a deal with him, and he opens in the play in a couple of weeks.'

It ran in the West End for eighteen months, and Leslie paid us – naturally – no commission.

Although Derek Nimmo carved out a career playing dippy clerics, there was nothing dippy about him in reality. He ran a very profitable company producing plays on a tight budget for expats in the Middle East. Ray Cooney in Abu Dhabi was just what they wanted to see.

I was in Sydney when Derek was starring in a play called *Why Not Stay for Breakfast?*. We met for the first time over dinner. He asked me what kind of deal I was on at my hotel. I explained that I was a guest of a film distribution company, so everything was being picked up. Derek's bill was also being paid, but theatrical producers work on rather tighter budgets.

'Do they pay for your laundry?' asked Derek.

'Well I guess they do, but I'm moving on to Hong Kong tomorrow, and I haven't really got any.'

'Do you mind if I put some of my laundry on your bill before you go?'

I was rather taken aback by this idea. I hardly knew Derek and wasn't desperately keen on getting acquainted with his laundry.

'What time's your flight?'

The following morning as I was eating breakfast in my room there was a knock on the door. It was the maid with an enormous basket of clothes.

'This is from Mr Nimmo,' she said.

A few minutes later there was another knock and a different maid.

'I believe you have some laundry, sir.'

She removed the basket. And when I signed the bill, there it all was, under sundries.

At the other end of the scale was Kenneth More. When Kenny More was in the early stages of Parkinson's disease, an illness that was to take his life far too quickly, he was offered a part in a film with which initially he thought he could cope; but the anxiety of it all made him change his mind and he had to withdraw. The producers were sympathetic, although I didn't go into much detail about his illness, as he was still hopeful of a recovery.

'The money would have been nice, darling,' he said to me. 'I'm sorry to have let you down.'

A few days later he wrote to me, saying how disappointed he was not to have been able to cope with the film and enclosed a cheque. I telephoned him and asked what the cheque was for.

'It's for your commission, darling,' he said. 'I don't see why you should be out of pocket just because I've had to pull out of the film.'

I tore the cheque up, not something I was in the habit of doing, but I never forgot his generosity. Sadly, he died soon afterwards at the tender age of sixty-seven.

In addition to our other duties, Julian and I had to buoy up our clients. Apart from a very few exceptions, actors enjoy working and when they're not working they need buoying up. Buoying up is an important part of the agent's stock-in-trade. I remember John Le Mesurier was in a play which was creaking to an early death in the West End, aided by some terrible notices and even worse performances. John had been out of work for months before the play opened and was counting on a decent run to sort out his ever-delicate finances. Unfortunately, the night I went to see him, the theatre was virtually empty and one or two of John's fellow performers were not quite on top of their lines. As I was ushered into his dressing room, I was struggling.

'What about you, then?' I said. (Always a good, though insincere, standby in an emergency.) John was the best thing in it, but that didn't really say much.

'Did you enjoy the play?' he asked. Now actors always ask you if you've enjoyed the play that they're in and the answer to give is obviously 'yes'. It's always best to be enthusiastic, but not overly so: Julian's rather over-the-top standby was 'It was the best play I've ever seen.' If I had used that one on John he would have thought I was taking the piss.

'I don't know what to say, John,' I replied. 'What an amazing evening.'

So far so good.

John then told me that the notice had gone up that evening and the play would be off by the end of the following week.

'Are there any other jobs in the pipeline?' he enquired. Of course, there weren't. I'd hoped he'd be in the play for at least six months, or maybe longer.

'Unfortunately not, but I'm sure once people hear you're free . . .'

I then had a flash of inspiration and remembered an apt phrase which a fellow agent had passed on to me. 'To be honest, John, I'm jolly pleased the play's coming off, because, to an extent, you're no good to me when you're working. I can't put you up for jobs; there are no contracts to negotiate; no photos and CVs to bike over to casting directors and producers. No deals to make. Do you know what your greatest asset is to me, John?'

'No,' he replied.

'Your availability!'

Before I left I spoke to Fred, the ninety-year-old stage doorman.

'It was quiet as a grave in there,' he said. 'And it's supposed to be a comedy, isn't it?'

Fred had been stage doorman for over seventy years and was renowned for these pithy *bons mots*. Producers would often let him read plays before they optioned them; after all, he'd seen a lot more of them than they had.

'You must have some amazing memories, Fred,' I said, 'all those years here, all those comedy legends. What were they like?'

'I saw 'em all, Michael,' he replied. 'Vesta Tilley, Little Titch, Marie Lloyd, Harry Lauder, the lot.' He paused. 'And shall I tell you something, Michael?'

'Yes, please, Fred.'

'Do you want me to be completely honest?'

'Yes, Fred.'

'They were all fucking awful. Every one of 'em. Give me that Richard Briers any day.'

Within a week of the play coming off, John had been offered another job. I think I had buoyed him up. I remember him telling me that his previous agent, Freddie Joachim, had told him, 'Don't make yourself too easy to get. Say no from time to time. It keeps producers on their toes.' That was all very well for Freddie, but John needed the work and hated turning things down. 'I always thought that Freddie viewed me as a Second XI client,' said John. 'On the very rare occasions he took me out to lunch it was never the Ivy, always the cafeteria at Bourne and Hollingsworth.'

John was the sweetest of men, tailor-made for the part of Sergeant Wilson in 'Dad's Army'. I remember working on a stall at a charity fête with him. A man pushed forward and pulled his sleeve.

'Are you who I think you are?' the man said. 'What's your name?'

'I'm sure it will come to you,' said John.

The man returned five minutes later. 'I know who you are!'

'Jolly good,' said John.

'You're Daphne du Maurier.'

'I'm afraid I'm not,' said John dejectedly, 'but I certainly wish I was.'

Another client, Donald Sinden, was also the master of the self-deprecating story. A favourite of mine was when he was working with Judi Dench at the RSC in Stratford, playing Benedick to her Beatrice in *Much Ado About Nothing*. The play opened to rave reviews and Donald was feeling very pleased with himself. Walking along the river on his way to the theatre one afternoon, two pretty girls approached him.

'Please, please may we have a photograph?'

Donald puffed out his chest.

'Of course. Where would you like it? In front of the theatre, or with the river and swans in the background?'

'By the river please.'

They walked to the river, chatting amiably about the fine spring weather.

'Here will be perfect,' said one of the girls.

Donald preened. The other girl handed him a camera. 'It's quite easy to operate. Just press this button.'

Donald took two photographs of the girls and then, somewhat deflated, headed for the stage door.

I discovered early on in our partnership that Julian kept rather eccentric hours. I quickly fell in with his routine, despite the potentially lethal consequences to my health. We would arrive in the office between 10.30 and 11 a.m., and have a cup of coffee together to discuss the day's social arrangements, which would usually include lunch at the Turf Club. It only dawned on me after a few months that our choice of offices in St James's Street was based entirely on their proximity to Carlton House Terrace. When I later suggested a move to Chelsea, our first lease having run out, Julian made me feel as though I'd suggested relocating to Peckham. At 12.45, Julian would saunter into my office to where the drinks cabinet was located – it was mutually agreed (and probably safer) that the cabinet would be located in my office, rather than his, as mine was the better office in which to entertain – and pour himself a large gin and tonic. We would then stroll down to the Turf, have a few drinks at the bar and settle down to lunch at 1.45. White wine with the starter, a carafe or two of red with our main course and cheese; then back to the bar for coffee and a couple of kümmels on the rocks, before returning to the office at around 3.30. Julian would then take a catnap or watch the racing on television. Cries of 'Come on my son!' would indicate that his investments were paying off; silence would suggest the opposite. From time to time the telephone would ring. At 5.45, Julian would return to the drinks cabinet for an early-evening scotch and then head back to the Turf for his evening's entertainment. I, on the other hand, would go home and place a damp towel across my head.

Needless to say, the Turf was Julian's second (and spiritual) home, where he was much loved and respected by members and staff. One year the Turf decided to convert some unwanted rooms into bedrooms, a transformation warmly received by the members. (No more expensive hotel rooms for country members, or long, drunken drives home after dinner.) Once the bedrooms were put into service, they proved so popular that the committee agreed to bend that most sacrosanct of rules and allow members' wives to share their husbands' rooms.

Seeking to take advantage of the new arrangements, Julian had a quiet word with the head porter, Grace, about the new accommodation.

'Does that mean we'll be able to bring our girlfriends to stay in the club, Grace?' asked Julian.

'Indeed, sir,' replied Grace, 'provided, of course, your girlfriend is the wife of a member.'

Julian put me up for the Turf, but I felt rather out of my depth there, having no particular interest in racing. Instead I joined the Garrick Club, which was more up my street. Don Taffner, the American television producer, once told me about a visit he had made to the Garrick. Two of the club's members had invited him to dinner, and as he arrived ahead of them, he was shown upstairs to the Morning Room. As he sat there alone, admiring the paintings, through the door walked Queen Elizabeth, the Queen Mother. Immediately, Don sprang to his feet. The Queen Mother, surprisingly unaccompanied, offered him an outstretched gloved hand.

'Don T–Taffner, Your M–Majesty,' he stuttered, attempting a bow.

'Good evening, Mr Taffner,' she replied, at which point two men appeared behind her.

'Ma'am, we're in the room next door.'

She gave Don a sweet smile and disappeared into an adjoining room, where she was attending a private party.

Over dinner Don found his two hosts on the patronizing side. 'I bet you don't have anything like this in New York?' 'What about these paintings, eh?' At the end of dinner Don said that his visit to the club had been a memorable occasion and one that he would always cherish. As they were walking from the dining room to the main entrance, the Queen Mother came down the stairs.

'Look Don, it's the Queen Mother,' whispered the member. 'She comes here quite often,' cooed his friend.

As she passed, she gave Don another gleaming smile.

'Good night, Mr Taffner,' she said.

'Good night, Ma'am,' he replied.

His hosts pulled themselves up from their deep bows and looked at him in amazement.

'What a great lady,' said Don.

As a lover of four-legged animals (slightly preferring them to the two-legged variety), Julian was keen that Leading Artists should be represented on the turf. *The Winner* and *Sporting Life* always took pride of place on the reception coffee table, well ahead of the *Hollywood Reporter* and *Screen International*. One day our accountant, Ron Parker, mentioned that we *might* be able to get some of the running costs of a racehorse through the company's advertising budget; but suggested that we should start on a smaller scale, perhaps with a greyhound. Julian, being a regular visitor to the Wimbledon dog track, was delighted. He met up with a trainer he knew called Randy Hamilton, and returned to the office with the news that we now owned a greyhound called 'Leading Artist'. The dog cost a modest sum — five hundred pounds —

but it clearly had a less than modest appetite, judging by the monthly food and board bills we paid. Leading Artist had never run professionally when Julian handed over our cash; so it was up to Randy to train the dog for a year and then decide if it would be good enough to race. Julian made a visit to Randy's training establishment somewhere in Essex and reported back that Leading Artist was looking fit and well.

'Did he know he was called Leading Artist?' I asked. 'Did he lick you like dogs do to their masters; was he pleased to see you?'

'Don't be ridiculous,' said Julian.

'What did he look like?' I asked.

'Like a bloody greyhound.'

'What, you mean grey and thin?'

'Exactly.'

'Well, judging by the amount of money Randy's charging us for food, I'm surprised he doesn't look like a fucking St Bernard. And, anyway, how did you know that it was Leading Artist and not just any old dog?'

'Well I didn't. But Randy was very positive, said he was doing really well and that by the end of the year we'd be in the winner's enclosure at Catford.'

Six months later Randy reported that Leading Artist hadn't made the grade after all; he was reluctantly going to have to put him out to grass. He submitted his final bill, which included a charge for rehousing, and we never

' "By the end of the year, we'll be in the winner's enclosure at Catford" '

heard from him again, not even a Christmas card. I wondered whether Leading Artist ever really existed, or was he the four-legged embodiment of all Randy's corporate clients owning a greyhound? Was Rover not only Leading Artist but also Curtis Brown, John Murray and William Morris? Had Julian fallen for the three-card trick like my father had with those doves?

The following year we bought a racehorse and Julian persuaded Nick Gaselee, one of the Royal Family's select group of trainers and a Turf Club chum of Julian's, to train it. Now we were into serious money. Randy wouldn't have been able to afford a hoof, let alone a leg. Up to this point, I had traditionally put a pound each way on a few of the horses in the Grand National in the vain hope that one would win, and left it at that. Now Julian moved me into a different league, into a world of 'yankees', 'bet doubles' and 'accumulators'. And the pound each way bet had turned into £100 to win. 'Put it on the nose,' Julian used to say. 'Each way is a loser's bet.' Julian endlessly told me what he had 'stood to win'. Sometimes it was £1,000, sometimes as much as £5,000. But I quickly realized that 'stood to win' meant that he had lost his original investment of several hundred pounds, so it wasn't quite as impressive as it sounded. Julian was always saying to me, 'Help yourself!' This meant that the bet was so rock solid that it would be churlish not to make a substantial investment. I fell for this kindness a couple of times, but without success, and then decided to leave Julian to help himself and leave me out of it.

Nevertheless, I did back Leading Artist — for that was his name — up to the hilt, until Julian told me *not* to help myself. Poor old Leading Artist had come nowhere in his first four starts and Nick Gaselee was recommending moving him on. His next start took him to Towcester, a race in which I was pleased not to have any financial involvement.

Over the weekend of the race, I was staying at the Blakeney Hotel in Norfolk (a far cheaper proposition than spending it at the races). Lying in my bath on Sunday morning, I took a cursory glance at the racing results and was surprised to see Leading Artist's name in bold print. What did this signify, I wondered? The answer was that the horse had won, and not just won, but had won at odds of 100 to 1. I leapt out of the bath and called Julian.

'It was fantastic,' he said. 'All the horses fell bar two and Leading Artist pissed up.' 'Pissed up' was another of Julian's favourite euphemisms. 'I took John Hurt with me and we both cleaned up. It was the first time a horse has won at 100 to 1 at Towcester since the 1930s.'

Sadly Leading Artist never won again, and Julian 'moved him on'.

To keep control of the ebb and flow of money coming in and going out of the office, an agency needs the services of an efficient bookkeeper. David Callaghan was an eccentric character and an excellent bookkeeper. He was efficient, hard-working, good at talking to actors and, most important of all, honest. After working with Terry Plunkett Greene and Julian, he worked for Leading Artists and ran the accounts department for many years before deciding he needed a change of scene. His departure gave Julian and me quite a shock: bookkeeping was certainly not our forte, and we tended to sign anything put in front of us.

Julian, however, had an even lower boredom threshold than I. His eyes would always glaze over during our company AGM, which he used to arrange at midday so that we could be at the Turf Club bar within the hour. After some searching, a lady called Yanka was engaged to take over from David. An intelligent, middle-aged woman, she had one major deficiency, which, it soon became clear, would end our relationship within weeks rather than the years for which I had hoped. Her problem was that she had a propensity for asking questions, to which Julian never knew the answer and cared even less.

'Do you keep the cashbook up to date on a daily or weekly basis?' she enquired.

'Do you sign one another's petty cash slips?'

'Do you like a mixture of notes and coins in the petty cash box?'

'Do you have a separate VAT account for your entertaining?'

'Do you mark personal items on your credit card bills?'

'Do you happen to know Daniel Day-Lewis's National Insurance number?'

'Is VAT payable on this contract?'

'Is Judi Dench a company and, if so, what is the registered number of the company?'

All perfectly reasonable, but this was an area of the business that held little appeal for me, and for Julian none at all. Indeed, it made him very cross. The more cross he became with poor Yanka, the more questions she asked, and her office was nearer to his than mine. She was endlessly walking in with ledgers, files and balance sheets, trying to get Julian's attention away from the 3.30 at Sandown – usually unsuccessfully. I used to keep my door firmly closed. If she ever happened to ease it open, I would grab both telephones off my desk and pretend I was on a hugely complicated three-way international conference call. 'Hang on a second, would you, Dimitri?'

It was clear that we would soon be talking of Yanka in the past tense. On one Friday afternoon, after Julian had had a particularly good lunch and was snoozing in his favourite armchair, Yanka walked into his office with a pile of VAT receipts she wanted to discuss with him.

Julian exploded. 'Madam, I have no interest whatsoever in your VAT receipts, or indeed in anything else you could possibly have to say to me. You're a crashing bore. I suggest you take your ledgers and your balance sheets and go fuck yourself!'

Yanka rushed into her office in floods of tears; moments later she was in front of my desk.

'I'm sure Julian didn't mean to be rude, Yanka. It's just that he does get easily bored with VAT.'

'I've done my best, but I can't take any more. I'm giving in my notice.'

I was hugely relieved, although the prospect of finding another bookkeeper filled me with horror.

'Oh really, Yanka? Well, of course, I do understand.'

Julian, of course, apologized to Yanka and even offered her a scotch, which, unsurprisingly, she declined. She left us a couple of weeks later.

'Christy Roche's sister,' said Julian. 'Perfect for us.'

Julian had been given the number of someone in Ireland who happened to know Christy Roche, whose sister just happened to be a bookkeeper.

'Really nice girl, lives in London, and is apparently looking for a bookkeeping job. We could have fallen on our feet here.'

I had no idea who Christy Roche was.

'Just one of the top Irish jockeys of all time, in my humble opinion,' said Julian. 'I think we're bloody lucky to have his sister working here.'

I wasn't sure that having a brother who was a top Irish jockey was necessarily a good thing in a bookkeeper – bookmaking maybe. Anyhow, the following morning Helen Roche arrived for an interview. After Julian had run through Christy's career, enquiring about his recent rides and any hot tips circulating around the Irish racing community, we got on to our requirements.

Helen was of leprechaun proportions and very Irish. She seemed to grasp immediately what was needed and, although she had never worked for a theatrical agency before, she had looked after the accounts of a number of small businesses both in England and in Ireland. She gave us the names and addresses of two referees, and told us she could start as soon as we needed her. She never mentioned VAT.

'Perfect,' said Julian, after she'd left. 'She's just what we're looking for. Let's offer her the job.'

'Shouldn't we check out her references first, just to see if she's any good?'

'Well do it quickly; we don't want to lose her.'

I telephoned her first referee, who gave her a sparkling review but turned out to be a relation rather than a former employer. The second referee had used her on a temporary basis in London and had found her honest and trustworthy. Julian was very eager to get everything fixed up; she seemed fine, given Yanka's sudden departure.

Helen could not have been more different from Yanka. Julian was certainly pleased; he would look through the accounts department glass door, smile at Helen and then beam at me. 'Wonderful. See the way she just gets on with it. Not all those bloody stupid questions that last woman kept asking.'

Indeed, Helen did get on with it. Her work was always efficient and well presented, and she quickly got the hang of how everything worked. At the end of each week she would bring in a large folder of cheques and statements for either Julian or me to sign. The cheques were mainly payable to our clients, less the agency commission; the rest payment of various bills and, of course, salary payments. Not complicated work, but requiring some expertise in the workings of an agency, which she seemed to acquire very quickly.

And then, after she had been with us for three months or so, she didn't appear in the office. I called her home number – she lived in a flat in Chiswick – which was answered by a man claiming to be a friend of hers. He said she was ill, but would call later in the day. No call.

The following morning I rang again, and there was no reply. One of the girls in the office said she would go round to her flat on her way home, but called me that evening to say there was nobody there. I rang Helen's number a couple of times that evening but still there was no reply. The following day, Julian got his racing contacts on to the case and heard back from Ireland, via Christy Roche, that he hadn't heard from his sister for some weeks but that she was working in London. Nobody had any contact numbers for her.

I now began to wonder whether Helen 'getting on with it' involved more than we had bargained for. I called our accountants and they came to the office straight away and went through all the books. Everything seemed to be in order. All the money had come in and gone out in the normal way. All cheques, signed by us, were payable either to known suppliers or named clients. Maybe we were being overly suspicious.

'Unlikely Christy Roche's sister would be on the fiddle,' said Julian.

And then, as Ron Parker had a final look through the books, the penny dropped. Well in fact £15,000. 'What she's done is clever,' said Ron, 'and, knowing your predilection for signing anything that's put under your noses, foolproof – if you'll pardon the expression – although only up to a point. She'd embarked on a scam that would ultimately be found out, though not for some time. I'm surprised she did a runner quite so soon.'

'So what exactly did she do?' asked Julian.

'Well, it's like this. As you know, you have two main accounts: your office account, which has all your commission in it, and your client account, which has all your clients' money in it. Every week your bookkeeper transfers your commission from the client to the office account, and then transfers all the client money to the artists in question. She presents you with the cheques to sign, made payable to the various clients. The cheques, from the office account, pay the salaries, bills, rent et cetera. When you were signing a cheque for £1,000 made payable, to say, Angela Thorne, you assumed, quite reasonably, that the money would be going from the client account into Angela Thorne's account. Often it was, but occasionally it was coming out of the office account. Therefore your money, and not hers, was going into Angela Thorne's account.'

'So was this just inefficiency?' Julian asked.

'Sadly, more than that, Julian,' said Ron. 'Because the Angela Thorne account wasn't the actress's account but an account opened in that name by Helen. She opened several accounts in various actors' names and, over a period of three months, managed to steal £15,000 of your money. So when you said "she just got on with it", Julian, that's precisely what she was doing. Getting on with stealing your money.'

'Well, at least she wasn't stealing our clients' money,' I said.

'If she'd done that, you would have found out very quickly. Actors tend to know when they have money due. You and Julian were a softer touch.'

'Charming,' said Julian.

Sometime later Helen was arrested for operating a similar fraud and ended up behind bars, but we never got our £15,000 back.

Our next bookkeeper was Stephen Scutt. His first few weeks were tricky, since Ron had told us to be more watchful about what we signed, and to show a bit more interest in the day-to-day running of the business.

So when Stephen would come into my office with a folder of statements with cheques attached for my signature, I was more exacting.

'Is this for a repeat?' I would ask.

'Yes,' Stephen would reply, 'from the BBC.'

'Where does it say BBC?'

'Here on the statement.' He would point to three huge capital letters saying 'BBC'.

'Four hundred and fifty pounds, eh? What was the original fee?'

'Well, I'd have to look at the statement from the BBC. Do you want me to?'

'Yes, maybe just to be on the safe side. And while you are at it, is that Dan's address?'

'Yes, as far as I know.'

'Has he moved recently?'

'I don't really know, Michael. I don't actually know who Dan is. Remember I've only been here a week, and the company I was with before imported leather goods from Spain.'

'Yes, of course. Well, I'll check that with Julian, but let me know what the original fee is.'

'Now what's this? John Hurt's profit participation in *The Elephant Man*? Is that all he's got? It should be much more than that.' And so it went on.

Of course, after a few weeks, things were back to normal, and Stephen was in and out of my office in the time it took Julian to pour himself a large gin and tonic.

Stephen ended up working for me for over twenty years, organizing the daily flow of monies in and monies out.

A bachelor, he lived in Chiswick and had a penchant for DIY. The most accident-prone person I ever met, he would arrive in the office with terrible stories of dreadful self-inflicted disasters, risking life and limb in the hopeless cause of do-it-yourself.

Like the time he decided to put up some wine racks to house the dozen bottles of vintage port that generous clients such as Richard Griffiths, Angela Thorne and Nigel Havers had given him over the years. He bought a wooden twelve-bottle wine rack and attempted to solve the problem of the lack of a cellar in his house by rather bizarrely putting this wine rack in his loft. One Sunday morning, with a casserole bubbling in the oven for his lunch, he opened the trapdoor of the attic and from the top of a ladder heaved his portly frame into the loft. He then fixed the rack to the wall with a series of nails and stood back to admire his handiwork. All very satisfactory. He then carefully carried up the bottles of Warre's 1970, Dow's '74, Taylor's '80 and Cockburn's '82, and placed them lovingly into the racks. He shut the trapdoor, removed the ladder and went downstairs to have his lunch.

As he removed the casserole from the oven, there was a loud crash and by the time he got back upstairs the top-floor ceiling was bright red and large dollops of port were dripping on to the carpet. He grabbed the ladder and, as he opened the loft door, port flooded out, covering him from head to foot. The rack had come off

223

the wall and lay dejectedly on the floor. The front doorbell rang. He looked out of the window. It was his elderly lady neighbour. As he opened the front door the woman screamed. He caught his reflection in the hall mirror. His hands were bright red and dripping with the port and he had a gash across his cheek from a piece of broken bottle. His neighbour didn't speak to him for months.

The port-stained floor gave him a good reason to have the house re-carpeted. He had lived there for ten years and it was in need of a freshen-up. Admiring the work of the carpet fitters after their departure, Stephen noticed they had not carpeted a small airing cupboard next to his bathroom and the bare boards offended him. With some of the off-cuts they had left behind, Stephen nailed down a strip of carpet, checked that everything was in order and decided he deserved a pre-lunch drink. Again this was a Sunday morning and his weekly casserole was simmering away. As he walked across his sitting room, a jet of boiling hot water shot across the room. This was quickly followed by another jet of water from the opposite side of the room, criss-crossing the first one, like some opulent water feature. Stephen was drenched. As the room began to steam up, he grabbed the telephone and rang his plumber. The plumber had just got back from the pub and was rather the worse for wear, but Stephen managed to talk him into coming over. The drunken plumber turned everything off and in an attempt to sober up joined him for a plate of his casserole. He subsequently discovered that Stephen had nailed through a vital pipe in the central heating system. What was this thing about Stephen and nails?

Nails came into play again a year or so later when he put up some shelves in the living room of his new house. The shelf unit between his kitchen and dining room was a large four-tiered affair in pine. Checking carefully that it was securely fastened, he filled it with books on three shelves and on the top fourth shelf placed his collection of rare porcelain figures. He stepped back yet again to admire his morning's work. The antique leather-bound books set off the delicate porcelain figures and his most prized possession, a Meissen harlequin, formed a fitting centrepiece for this elegant display. He went into the kitchen, closing the door behind him; the oven was smoking and he didn't want cooking smells in the sitting room, as he had friends coming for tea. As he lifted the casserole on to the kitchen table and started to serve himself with a generous portion, there was a deafening crash from outside the door. He pushed the door but it wouldn't open. The shelves had fallen off the wall on to the floor, followed by the books and porcelain, and had banked up against the door. He climbed out of the window but had no latch key to get him back into the house, so he was forced to smash a window into the sitting room, where he was confronted by the full horror of his hopeless handiwork.

The loss of his porcelain collection forced Stephen into abandoning his DIY aspirations once and for all. Leave it to the experts would be his motto. Well, apart from fixing to the wall of the garage his father's antique Victorian toolbox, which had sat gathering dust on the floor for many years. He fixed two smart brass brackets on to the plugged walls and then lifted the heavy box on to them. It looked very handsome and he was glad that for once he had used screws rather than nails. As he leant back to get a good look at the whole effect, the box sprang off the brackets and hit him on the chest, forcing him back on to the bonnet of his car. He struggled to free himself and as he slipped from beneath the box, he saw it crash down on to the bonnet, causing what subsequently turned out to be over £1,000 worth of damage. He also discovered that he had two badly cracked ribs and it was several weeks before he was able to lift another casserole dish into the oven.

By the summer of 1985, I was beginning to tread water again: was it time to move on? I was finding that one of the problems with being an actors' agent was the almost total lack of any direct involvement in the creative process. OK, so you'd read the odd script and give the actor your opinion as to its merits, but that was about the full extent of it. Although I wanted to carry on as an agent, I also wanted to become involved in the production side of the business, developing ideas and scripts for

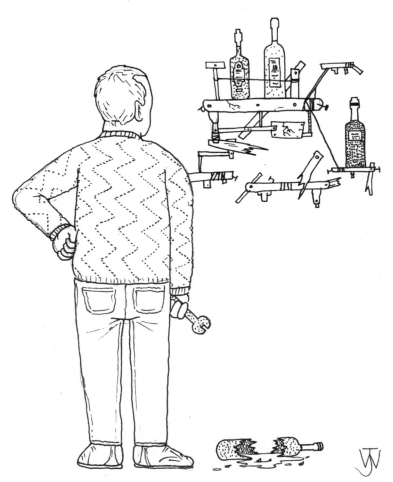

'A bachelor with a penchant for DIY'

television and presenting plays for the theatre. I discussed my aspirations with Julian. Would he also be interested in getting involved with that side of the business?

'Not my cup of tea, old boy,' he said. 'Conflict of interest: you can't be an agent and a producer. Wouldn't work. All the clients would leave.'

I thought this was a rather sweeping appraisal of the situation, though Julian's response was not unexpected. He found being an agent professionally fulfilling. I, on the other hand, didn't, even though actors were more integral to my personal life than to his.

My friends tended to be, if not my clients, then certainly people in or around the business. Julian was completely different. 'I simply can't understand how anyone could possibly want to see Peter Bowles on a *Sunday*,' he'd say, with incredulity. His friends were mainly fellow members of the Turf Club, racing people or those with an interest in horseracing. He had good relationships with his clients, and would defend them to the hilt; but evenings (apart from first nights) and weekends were his time, not theirs.

Julian most probably had it right. Even as their agent, I sometimes expected my clients to be like the characters they played on stage and screen. Some were, but most weren't. The suave, sophisticated matinee idol is usually racked with insecurities, not remotely sophisticated, and invariably a lot less suave than he pretends to be. Comedy actors seldom sit around dinner tables cracking jokes. And the hard man of films and television drama is often a softy underneath. Actors tend to be mercurial, multi-layered people, like those Russian dolls, and one never quite knows whether one is talking to the real person or whether there are a few more layers underneath.

David Lean thought too much intelligence in an actor was a bad thing. When he was making *A Passage to India* with Nigel Havers and James Fox, he was directing a long shot of Peggy Ashcroft outside the Marabar caves. He wanted her to look across towards the cave and point. He sent her a message via his first assistant. The response came back from her on the walky-talky, 'Dame Peggy wants to know *why* she is pointing towards the cave.' David blew his top, and told his first assistant to tell her that David wants her to point at the cave because he's told her to, and she's a fucking actress and he's the fucking director. The diplomatic first assistant presented Sir David's compliments to Dame Peggy and said it would help him hugely with a linking shot later in the sequence. 'God protect me from intelligent actors. All one wants is for them to be able to act and do as they're fucking told,' said David.

I had been with Julian for ten very happy and profitable years, but I felt I needed a few new challenges and my liver was also telling me it was time for a change. I dreaded telling Julian, as I knew he'd find it incomprehensible, which he did. The divorce was amicable: no custody battles over clients and no alimony payments. It was pretty clear who was going with whom; the financial side of the business was divided neatly; and Julian was happy to take over the lease of 60 St James's Street. I was equally happy to flee the temptations of St James's and start leading a more sheltered existence in South Kensington.

Our assistant, Amanda Fitzalan Howard, came with me, as did Stephen Scutt, although I declined his offer to help with the refurbishment of the new offices at 125 Gloucester Road, next door to the Gloucester Road Bookshop. The day we moved in I noticed a book, which I subsequently bought, in the shop window; it was *A Madman's Musings* by 'A Patient during his Detention in a Private Madhouse'. Was this an omen?

9

They Come, They Go, Who Called?

Hanging pictures, either at home or in the office, is always a priority. I've even, from time to time, hung pictures for other people. Buying a good picture is easy; hanging it more difficult. I remember being taken by Elaine Stritch to meet Ava Gardner at her flat in South Kensington.

'Nowadays, she doesn't look like she did in *The Barefoot Contessa*,' said Elaine, 'but she's a great girl.'

And she certainly was. By now in her sixties, Ava had a deep sexy voice, and I readily agreed to join her in a champagne cocktail, even though it was four o'clock in the afternoon. Her flat was exquisitely furnished, and I noticed a small painting tucked away in a dark corner on the stairs. On closer inspection it looked like one of Picasso's early pastel drawings.

'Is that a Picasso?' I asked.

'Yes, darling,' she replied, 'I bought it in New York. It's of a model Picasso had a fling with in Paris. Her name's on the back.'

'Why have you hidden it away on the stairs?'

'To be honest, darling, there just happened to be a nail there.'

There were no nails on the walls of 125 Gloucester Road when we moved in, so everything had to be carefully measured out. I was hanging a pair of piscatorial prints in the loo when I was reminded of the trouble Nigel Havers got into, having bought a fish painting (much grander than my humble engravings) from a dealer. Nigel was very excited with his purchase, which he told me the dealer had let him have for £5,000, less than cost price. This sounded on the steep side to me, but it was of a style and period of painting I knew nothing about and took Nigel's word for it, although in my experience, art dealers seldom sell you pictures for less than they have paid for them.

After a few months, the colour supplement of a Sunday newspaper ran a feature on the Haverses at home, and there on the front cover of the magazine was a photograph of them standing proudly in front of their sitting-room fireplace, with the fish picture above the mantelpiece. The following day I had an agitated Nigel on the phone.

'The police have just been round to the house and have taken my fish painting away. It's apparently on the stolen paintings register and the owner spotted it in the magazine.'

I suggested that Nigel contact the dealer, who was on holiday in France, and see what light he could shed on the matter. The dealer, of course, had no idea the painting was stolen; he'd got it from a runner who said he'd bought it in an auction room up North. The police verified that the painting did indeed belong to the previous owner and Nigel was advised that the only person he could look to for compensation was the dealer. So Nigel had another chat with his friend, now back from France, who agreed to pay him £2,000, the purchase price of the picture.

'But you told me you'd paid £5,000 for it.'

'Well, when I said cost price, I obviously had to cover my overheads. The picture would have been twice that anywhere else. You got a bargain, Nige.'

Nigel didn't want to fall out with his dealer, so he accepted the money and it was never mentioned again.

Some months later, Dorothy Tutin rang me.

'I know you collect paintings,' she said.

'Indeed I do.'

'You know my mother wore a glass eye . . .'

Indeed I didn't, but I was grasping for the link between these two remarks. Perhaps she had a portrait of her mother to sell.

'Well . . . she had a collection of them, six in all, in a wooden box.'

Right. Why six? Surely one is enough in the glass eye world, or do you swap them around a bit as the mood takes you? The only trouble is that presumably they have to be a perfect match with the non–glass eye, so they must all be the same. Surely both her eyes weren't glass?

'I'm sure you go to a lot of auctions. Do you think a box of glass eyes in very good condition might be worth anything?'

'To a specialist glass eye collector, maybe,' I replied. 'But I'm not very strong in that department, being more of a modern British paintings man myself.'

I promised to look into it for her, which I'm ashamed to say I never did. I wonder what became of that wooden box of six shiny glass eyes?

Now that I was running a smaller stable than I had with Julian, I needed to maintain an even closer personal relationship with my clients. They had my home numbers and would call me out of office hours if they had a problem. 'Sorry to call you on a Sunday, Michael, but do you think I'll ever work again?' – that kind of thing. One even called me on a Sunday evening and said she was going to kill herself.

I went to their houses and they came to mine. I got to know their families and friends; went to their weddings and funerals; was godfather to their children; witnessed their wills (though seldom was I a beneficiary); and even stood as best man at their weddings. They became friends, although friends of an unconventional kind. I was always aware that there was work to look after, and if that aspect of their life started to show signs of wear and tear, the friendship might follow suit.

Although the agent is generally thought of as the tough, ruthless member of the partnership, with the actor portrayed as the gifted, vulnerable party, when it comes to being given the sack, it is virtually unheard of for the agent to wield the knife. I only ever sacked one actor, for being rude to my secretary on an almost daily basis. Needless to say, he was charming to me. In the end I realized I needed her a lot more than I needed him. But usually the agent waits to be sacked by the actor and can usually sense when the sack is in the air.

The letter, if indeed dismissal is by letter (faxes and e-mails are more common nowadays; the personal visit to the office is rare, and the goodbye lunch at Sheekey's a collector's item) includes gratitude for all you have done (it's usually because he thinks you've done so little that the actor is leaving), insists on telling you how difficult a decision leaving has been (sticking a stamp on an envelope and putting it in a letter box is never easy) and closes with the fond hope that he will remain good friends with you. 'I hope this will not in any way affect our friendship, which I value more than anything.' (But, of course, it always does.) Once an actress left me and forgot to tell me. I was watching the television one evening and there she was, playing her heart out in a medical drama about a sex-change clinic.

'Did we do the deal for that?' I asked my assistant the following morning. We hadn't and indeed nobody in the office, including me, had spoken to her for several months. At least she could have called and left a message on the answering machine.

In his memoir, *Bring on the Empty Horses*, David Niven tells a story about an actor whose career had prospered under the guiding hand of a much-respected agent. They had been together for many years, and their business relationship had developed into a close personal friendship. One evening, at a glamorous party, the actor met a big-league agent called Bert Allenberg who represented some of Hollywood's top stars. The actor was amazed when Allenberg asked to represent him. Amazed but, like most actors, susceptible to flattery. During a sleepless night, he weighed his ambition and greed against his integrity.

He met his agent the following morning and broke the news that he was leaving him.

'But why?' asked the agent.

'It's nothing personal, it's just . . .'

The agent told him that he was the first actor that he had ever *really* liked and ever *really* trusted; but now he knew that he was just the same, like all the rest. He was never going to represent an actor again.

'He'll get over it,' said Allenberg, opening a bottle of champagne while outlining his plans for the actor's career. He had some important meetings about him over the following few days, and asked the actor to call him on Wednesday morning.

In a state of high anticipation, the actor telephoned Allenberg's office. The secretary's voice was laboured. 'Mr Allenberg died last night,' she sobbed.

The actor was David Niven.

Niven obviously thought that actors' careers are somehow created by their agents. I've never been so sure about that: I'm not even sure whether actors really have careers, in the sense of a career being planned. If you leave school and become a chartered accountant, you can to some extent map out a career path that ultimately leads to being on the board of some listed company that will pay you large sums of money for looking after their large sums of money.

Actors have a string of jobs and with any luck these will follow each other in reasonably quick succession. The trick is to turn down the ones that don't move you forward, even if you need the money. That nice small part tends only to lead to more nice small parts and the I-might-as-well-do-it-I'm-not-doing-anything-else job is usually not that good an idea. But sadly actors (and indeed their agents) are not really controlling the game. The business is a mercurial affair, and the slippery slope downwards always seems to be a lot busier than the one going up.

There are, of course, far fewer decent acting jobs in film, television and theatre these days. Once upon a time, if you were good-looking and talented, the way to the stars was a relatively straightforward affair; although staying there was difficult. Actors could get away with being 'difficult', 'slow studies' or 'best before lunch'. But these days everyone has to be squeaky clean and there are very few actors who can guarantee ticket sales any more. On screen perhaps a handful, and the same on television, but in the theatre if you haven't got Dame Judi Dench or Dame Maggie Smith don't count on it. 'The business has changed' is a hoary old theatrical cliché, but none the less true.

In his book *With Nails*, Richard E. Grant tells his version of how he got the part of Withnail in *Withnail and I*. He described our first meeting, when I was 'immaculately dressed in a Pringle cardigan'. I have never worn anything from Pringle, and have certainly never worn a cardigan. Could anyone in such a get-up be considered 'immaculately dressed'? I doubt it.

But the Richard E. Grant story – which took place just as I'd set up on my own – is an interesting one about agents, actors and the film business. I remember it like this.

Richard Cottrell, who ran the Bristol Old Vic and was a client of ours, asked Julian and me to come and see a production of *Dracula* with a young actor who had been at the Bristol Old Vic Drama School and who he thought was very interesting. His name was Daniel Day-Lewis. There was no doubt that this charmingly eccentric young man had talent, so we swiftly took him on. After doing various TV jobs, we were sent a script for Dan called *My*

Beautiful Laundrette. Julian hated it. I hated it. Dan loved it. We advised him not to do it. He said he wanted to. He did it. It was a huge success and put him on the road to movie stardom. So much for our expertise in guiding young actors' careers.

Soon other scripts were heading in his direction and a copy of Bruce Robinson's *Withnail and I* landed on our desk. I thought it was a rather in-joke piece, clearly written by an actor and likely to appeal to actors but probably not to many other people. Dan loved it and we were in the process of negotiating a deal for him to play Withnail when a script of William Boyd's book *Stars and Bars* appeared. I greatly enjoyed the book but found the script disappointing. Dan loved it and wanted to do it. Unfortunately, the dates clashed with *Withnail* so we had to choose one or the other. We went for *Withnail*, Dan went for *Stars and Bars*, and so we had to call the casting director Mary Selway and get him out of *Withnail*. The director, the producer and even the executive producer, George Harrison, were all furious with us, of course. We had sabotaged their film. We had obviously talked Dan into doing *Stars and Bars* because the money was better. Typical agents. I had already set Richard Griffiths to play Uncle Monty, but they'd forgotten that. Mary wanted me to ask Colin Firth whether he would be interested in the part, even though he was totally wrong for it and unavailable. I assured her that he wasn't available. Mary went off to find another actor, and I moved off to Gloucester Road.

David Conville, who ran the Regent's Park Open Air Theatre and was a friend, called to ask me if I would meet a young actor who was looking for an agent. His track record didn't sound very exciting. Born and bought up in Swaziland, he'd been in England for three years and done bits and pieces of theatre and a BBC television play. Out of politeness to David, I said I'd see him.

Richard E. Grant was an oddish name, I thought, but there was already an actor called Richard Grant, hence the addition of the E, the first letter of his real surname. All very confusing. He sat on my sofa looking gangly and nervous, and handed me a tape of Les Blair's television drama *Honest Decent and True*. I promised to look at it and get back to him. I took the tape home that evening and, after dinner, watched ten minutes of it, fell asleep, woke up and went to bed. The next morning Hilary said it was rather good and she thought Richard was interesting. So, much to his delight, I took him on.

A week later, Mary Selway rang me to confirm that Daniel was definitely doing *Stars and Bars* and Colin was definitely unavailable. Did I have anyone else? Bruce was desperate; shooting started in a month or so.

'What about Richard E. Grant?' I said.

'Who?'

'Richard E. Grant.'

'Who the hell is Richard E. Grant? Come off it, Michael, you're making it up.'

'He's a new client, very talented. Great in the new Les Blair film, done some interesting stage work too.'

'We need a name.'

'Why not make one?'

'I'll get back to you, Michael. I suppose there's no chance of Colin changing his mind?'

'He's not available, Mary.'

I sent Mary a photograph of Richard with his rather skimpy CV and heard nothing. Then Bruce came on the phone.

'Are you *trying* to fuck up my film? You talk Dan Day-Lewis into doing a shit film like *Stars and Bars*, make up some crap Colin Firth is supposed to be filming and then offer us some prick called Robert E. Grant.'

'Richard actually, Bruce. You should meet him; he's perfect for the part, right look, right age.'

After several meetings, readings and screen tests Mary called me to offer Richard the part. He was ecstatic. I was the best agent in the world. He thanked God for the day he met me, and that I'd enjoyed the Les Blair so much. And thank God that David Conville called me. When did he start?

'Well, I have to do your deal.'

'My deal. But I'll do it for nothing.'

'Probably not best for me to tell them that.'

'But I will.'

Mary offered him a terrible deal for ten weeks' filming, plus two free weeks, plus free post-sync, plus free travel and plus free everything. A truly appalling offer.

'Nobody knows who he is,' said Mary. 'George Harrison has never heard of him.'

'Really, Mary, that does surprise me. Hasn't George ever been to the theatre?'

'Not in Swaziland he hasn't,' said Mary.

'Well he's not doing it for that. As it's a low–budget film and his first part, I'll take three times that for the picture plus a percentage.'

'No way.'

'You wouldn't have paid Dan or Colin anything like that.'

'Why, are they available?'

'*No*, Mary.'

Mary came back the following day and offered me double her original offer. I rang Richard.

'I'll do it for nothing.'

'Richard, it's the wrong money. I know they'll go to more.'

'Don't lose it.'

Richard rang back. Bruce had called him to say that was the top offer. I called Bruce and told him to go and fuck himself or something along those lines. Mary agreed it was wholly unprofessional of Bruce to call Richard and apologized. They'd go to my figure, but no percentage. I had never expected a percentage anyway. I was delighted, Richard even more so, and relieved, I guess, that I hadn't 'lost it'.

The film was a quiet success, but not of cult status; that came later. Richard was offered another Bruce Robinson movie, *How to Get Ahead in Advertising*, which had Richard's character developing a boil on his neck which turns into a second head. I hated the script and told Richard not to do it. He said Bruce thought it was wonderful and would make Richard a big star. I said he would say that, wouldn't he, as he wrote it and was directing it.

Richard did the film and it was a disaster. He then went to Los Angeles to do a film called *Warlock* (another turkey) and met an American agent who wanted to represent him worldwide and wanted 10 per cent commission. Richard didn't think that would be a problem. I did. I talked to the guy on the telephone; he was a schmuck. Richard called me and accused me of being rude to him.

'But he's a schmuck,' I said.

'You say one thing, and he says another,' said Richard. 'I just don't know who to believe.'

'But you've only met this guy once.'

'I know, but it's really difficult to know who to believe.'

'If you don't know who to believe, Richard, then I think it's time you moved on. I'll send your files over to your home in the morning.'

Did Richard then thank God for the day he met Bernie Goldshaft, or whoever his name was? Probably. As the William Morris agent said to his secretary on arriving at his office to find a letter from a star client giving him the sack: 'They come, they go, who called?'

★ ★ ★

A lesson I continued not to learn in the agency business was if a producer, director or whoever has a complaint about an actor while they're working, don't allow yourself to get into the middle, which of course is where the producer would like you to be. So when you get the call to say your client is throwing tantrums; refusing to strip as per contract; won't come out of his caravan; is drunk, is stoned; can't remember his lines; has put on a stone since his costume fitting; can't speak a word of French when he said he was practically bilingual; has disappeared; is late on the set every day or is just generally a total pain in the arse; you, as the agent, must say to the producer, 'You talk to them. It's not my job. I just do the deals.'

But one never does this, and so something along the following lines happens and you end up losing both your cool and your client.

The actor arrives on set drunk – well, according to the producer, anyhow.

'And it's not the first time,' says the producer on the telephone. 'The director say's he's hardly ever sober.'

'I'm amazed,' I say, 'I've never heard of him drinking when he's working. Come to think of it, I didn't even know he drank.' (OK, not quite true, but I *am* his agent.)

'Will you have a word with him?' asks the producer.

'I think it would be better if *you* have a word,' I reply. 'After all, you're the one there.' (He's filming on a distant location and I'm at home in London.)

'Well, I'm not actually there either,' says the producer. 'The director says that he's virtually unfilmable after lunch.'

'Well, why doesn't the director have a word with him?' I suggest.

'He doesn't think it's his job.'

'Do you?' I ask.

'No, not really. I've talked to him about it and he thinks *you* should speak to him.'

'I bet he does.'

'Well, you never mentioned his drinking when you suggested him for the part,' says the producer.

'Oh great,' I reply. 'You mean when I said how good he'd be as the Bishop of Bath and Wells, I should have added, "But don't forget he's a big boozer, so don't schedule any of his scenes after lunch."'

'Well, I'm sorry, Michael, but we all think *you* should talk to him and we'd be grateful if you would do it sooner rather than later.'

So, I make the call.

'How are you?'

'Fine, Michael.'

'How's the film going?'

'Great.'

'How's Loch Lomond?'

'Very nice.'

'So?'

'Yes?'

'I've had a call from Gerry.'

'Oh yes?'

'He says you're doing really well and they're all really pleased with the rushes.'

'Good.'

'But the director says that on a couple of occasions you look as though you might have had a drink with lunch.'

'What?'

'Look, I know. You – drinking when you're working. No way.'

'We've got to nail this, Michael. Tell them to fuck off.'

I then realize that he's drunk.

'Look, maybe you should just cool it a bit.'

'Cool what?'

'You know, the drinking.'

'Oh, so you're on their side, are you?'

'No.'

'So why are you believing them and not me? They say I'm drinking. I say I'm not. So who do you believe?'

Now it starts to get tricky.

'Well, I can't believe that Gerry would ring me if there was nothing wrong.'

'So, you believe *him*?'

'No, I'm not saying that, I'm just saying that . . .'

'Just fuck off. If my agent doesn't believe me and believes some two-bit film producer and second-rate director, then I need another fucking agent.'

'Maybe you do.'

'Oh great, so you're sacking me.'

'No, *you're* sacking me.'

'After all these years, I thought we were friends. You told me once that I was your favourite client.'

'That's got nothing to do with it.'

'No, clearly not. Well, you've obviously made up your mind, so I might as well fuck off. Thanks for your support.'

End of telephone call – end of friendship – client lost.

Nowadays actors, apart from a notorious few, never have a drink before going on stage. Several afterwards, but none before. But once upon a time, things were very different. The legendary actor (and drinker) Wilfred Lawson was playing Richard III on a provincial tour and got well tanked up at the pub next door prior to the opening night in Chelmsford, with a fellow actor who was playing the Duke of Buckingham.

Staggering on to the stage, he had some difficulty in keeping his balance. When he began Richard's big speech – 'Now is the winter of our discontent' – he was barracked by a man in the dress circle.

'You're drunk!' the man shouted.

Lawson carried on regardless.

'Made more glorious by . . .'

By now several other members of the audience had joined in.

'Get off, you're pissed!'

Lawson stopped, held himself steady, pushed out his chest, and in a loud and clear voice said, 'If you think *I'm* pissed, wait till you see the Duke of Buckingham!'

One of the most anecdotally rich actresses I ever looked after was Elaine Stritch. She had the most wonderful sense of humour: she once described a production of *A Month in the Country* at the National Theatre as so boring 'it felt more like six months in the country'. Although for many years a big star of musicals, she became a TV star in Britain, following the success of 'Two's Company' with Donald Sinden. Michael Grade, then Controller of Programmes at LWT, rang me and asked if I would be interested in representing Elaine. She was unhappy with her agent and had asked Michael to recommend someone else. He set up a meeting, and she joined me a few weeks later; although she forgot to tell her previous agent until he noticed that some residual payments had been diverted to me. Elaine was then living at the Savoy, where she had a grace-and-favour suite. She was driven around in a white Rolls-Royce and, like the Queen, never seemed to carry money with her.

She rang me one morning to say that she had been invited to a party at Bob Monkhouse's house in Bedfordshire, and would I like to join her. The following Sunday morning I showed up outside the Savoy at 11.30, and we headed off to the country.

'I'm not sure why Bob's asked me; I hardly know him. But it should be fun,' she said.

I certainly didn't know Bob and wasn't so sure about the fun element. I couldn't have been more right. The place was heaving with people: Petula Clark, Johnny Dankworth, Cleo Laine and Fenella Fielding were all huddled around the buffet table.

'Let me introduce you to Anita Harris,' said Elaine, 'she's a real darling.'

'Do you know Rod Hull?' said Anita. 'It's Michael White, isn't it?'

As I munched on a sausage roll, trying desperately to avoid eye contact with Bernie Winters, Clive Dunn grabbed my arm.

'What are you doing here?' asked Clive. 'I didn't know you knew Bob.'

'Well, I don't actually. I'm with Elaine Stritch.'

Clive was a new client of mine; he worked on the cusp of the legit world and had become famous through 'Dad's Army'.

'I'll introduce you to Bob; you'll love him.' He disappeared with a group of women who looked suspiciously like the Beverley Sisters. Elaine returned from having a long conversation with Ted Rogers, who she thought was a singer.

'I don't know about you, Elaine,' I said, 'but I wouldn't mind heading back.'

'I'd love to, darling, but we can't go until six o'clock.'

'Six o'clock! It's only a quarter past one. That's nearly five hours away. Why?'

'Well, the thing is . . .' And Elaine explained that in order to keep running the Rolls, she had to rent it out as much as she could. Sunday was always a busy day and her chauffeur was currently taking a group of Japanese tourists around London. They'd probably be at the Tower of London by now.

'So why six o'clock?' I asked.

'We usually do two tours on a Sunday. He's dropping off the Japanese about three, and then picking up some Germans at the Savoy and taking them to Hampton Court.'

The post-lunch arrivals included Bernard Bresslaw, who told me that he was a great admirer of Elaine's and would love to work with her in something. Then there were speeches – it was someone's birthday – followed by tea on the lawn. I fell into conversation with a variety agent, who had a list of comics and singers whose careers were either dead or in their death throes.

'One of my clients is very keen to get into legit work,' he said. 'He's done sketches with proper actors like Bill Pertwee and June Whitfield. Can I get him to call you? Do you have a card?'

I didn't have a card and never have had, and certainly did not want his client ringing me.

'Would I know him?' I asked, trying to look interested.

'Do you ever do the northern clubs?' he asked.

'To be honest, no,' I replied. 'The Royal Exchange in Manchester is as about as far north as I go.'

'I don't know that one. But getting back to my boy, he's a sort of singing Albert Finney, if you know what I mean. Good-looking in a rough diamond sort of way – loads of charisma.'

He handed me his card, which was in the shape of a star, edged in silver. 'I'll get your number from Bob and have Norman call you,' and he disappeared into a marquee.

I never heard from Norman. Maybe Bob didn't have my number (he certainly didn't have my name), although I did wonder who it was. Norman Wisdom perhaps, or Norman Vaughan: neither dead-ringers for Albert Finney, but Norman Wisdom did have a nice light singing voice. I lost the star-shaped card when I was looking for a back-up telephone number for a cab company, as the cucumber sandwiches were starting to curl on the lawn.

'The car's held up in traffic, darling,' said Elaine. 'The Germans were late so the driver didn't get away until five.'

People were beginning to drift off. Lots of hugging and kissing. Roy Hudd asked me for directions to the loo. I'd killed quite a bit of time there during the afternoon, so I was able to point him in the right direction. And then, at last, the Rolls appeared.

'OK, darling, we're off. I've said my goodbyes. Bob said he's really sorry to have missed you. Did you have fun?' asked Elaine.

251

'Yes,' I replied, 'it was really nice to meet Rod Hull, even though he didn't have Emu with him.'

And with that we headed through the Bedfordshire countryside back to the Savoy.

An invitation to dine with Elaine was always a traumatic experience.

'Come to my suite at the Savoy around eight.' On arrival, the conversation would follow a predictable pattern.

'Where would you like to eat, darling?'

'Wherever, Elaine, you choose.' It was after all her invitation.

'Luigi, darling,' she would say down the telephone, 'it's Elaine Stritch. Do you have a table for two in twenty minutes? Great.' And then a pause. 'Will it be complimentary?' Another pause. 'OK . . . I see . . . right. I'll leave it.'

The telephone would go down.

'Cheapskates.' She redialled.

'Antonio. Hi, darling . . .'

And so on. Her perseverance would usually lead to a complimentary dinner somewhere, often at a restaurant called Thomas de Quincey in Covent Garden, which, I believe, ultimately went bust.

When Elaine finally left the Savoy, she asked me to join her for supper in the Grill Room. As we sat in the bar having coffee after an excellent (and presumably complimentary) meal, she produced a large parcel.

'Darling, I have a present for you; to thank you for all you've done for me over the last few years.'

I was flattered that Elaine had gone to the trouble of buying me a present, let alone wrapping it so elegantly. I was hugely fond of her, and this thoughtfulness made me even more so.

I made to open the package.

'Don't open it here!' she shrieked. And then more quietly, 'Open it when you get home, darling.'

After fond farewells, I took a cab home and, before going to bed, pulled the wrapping paper off the parcel, to reveal a large, soft white bath towel with 'Savoy Hotel' embroidered on the corner.

Whereas with Elaine one rarely knew in advance where one would eat, with another client, Edward Fox, one occasionally doubted whether one was going to eat at all. Edward had been a good friend for many years; I met him on my first day at ICM, when his father, Robin, introduced us. One evening, during my bachelor days, he invited me to an impromptu supper at his house. As my Bird's Eye Fisherman's Pie hadn't yet reached the oven, I set off for Maida Vale. There didn't seem to be much activity in Edward's kitchen, even though it was nearly nine o'clock.

'What would you like to eat?' he asked, opening the fridge and parading a selection of rather unappetizing items in front of me. We settled on a cheese salad, which he would put together after we'd had a drink. We moved into the sitting room. A silver tray of bottles stood on a table in the corner of the room and from it Edward produced a bottle of gin.

'Gin and tonic?' he asked.

'Do you have any vodka?'

'Sorry, old boy.'

'Gin will be fine,' I said.

The bottle had a label on it, which, I guessed, had been discontinued a decade ago. But nothing wrong with vintage gin, I thought. He returned from the kitchen with the news that there was no tonic water apart from a bottle which had been open for a few weeks. Despite Edward's encouraging shakes, the tonic failed to produce any fizz. I declined neat gin, and Edward then produced a bottle of Marsala, some Blue Curaçao, and a half-bottle of Kirsch. As pre-supper cocktails, these didn't seem to fit the bill.

'What about a glass of wine?' he asked. 'Red or white?'

After a brief hiatus, Edward returned again from the kitchen. 'Damn, no wine.'

With the prospect of a glass of tap water looming, I suggested that I go to the off-licence and get in some supplies. 'Wouldn't hear of it,' said my host. 'I've got plenty of wine. I'll go and get a bottle,' and he headed down the stairs. Rather than risk having to make the cheese salad, I followed him and was surprised to see him walking through the front door and into his car, rather than down to the cellar. We drove off along Warwick Avenue and headed north up Maida Vale. It was now nearly ten o'clock and I was feeling very hungry and very thirsty.

Somewhere in Kilburn, we turned into a dark side street of lock-up garages and Edward pulled up in front of one of them. He fumbled with some keys in the darkness and pulled up the metal door to reveal more darkness.

'Damn lightbulb's down. Stay there.' Edward disappeared into the gloom and I then made out the shape of some boxes at the end of the garage. 'Red or white?' he shouted.

'White for me, please,' I replied.

He returned with a single bottle of white Chardonnay.

'As we're here, Edward, might it be worth taking back a couple of bottles? And maybe a couple of reds?'

'Bloody good idea,' he said.

Back in the car and on the way home, I noticed it was now 10.30 p.m. and I was beginning to go off the boil from a food point of view. Nevertheless, once we were back in Edward's cosy kitchen a cheddar cheese salad washed down with a few glasses of warm Chardonnay soon lifted my spirits. We never got to the red.

Around this time, Martin Jarvis was rehearsing a play and having problems. He just couldn't get to grips with the part; his co-star was impossible and he didn't think the director liked him. He was starting to get paranoid about the whole thing, although of course, to the outside world, he was his usual cool and charming self. Every morning and evening, he would give the receptionist in his hotel a cheery greeting and, more often than not, stop for a chat.

'How's the play going, Mr Jarvis?'

'Really well, thank you, Sandra.'

'We can't wait to see it. You're so clever, you actors. How do you remember your lines?' That kind of thing.

'I'll put some tickets aside for you,' cooed Martin.

What a nice man, she thought, so normal.

After the dress rehearsal, which had not gone well, he returned to his hotel, his nerves in tatters.

'Good evening, Mr Jarvis.' Martin gave the receptionist a big smile. 'Everything going well?'

'Wonderfully well,' said Martin as he headed for the lift.

Later in the evening, after a room service supper, which he couldn't eat, he lay on his bed worrying. The play didn't work. He wasn't any good. Should he take a sleeping pill? Should he take the whole bottle? He grabbed the phone and rang his wife. Before she'd had a chance to say hello, Martin told her everything.

'I can't take any more of this. The director's a nightmare, and I can't get the lines into my thick skull, not that they're worth learning anyway. The whole thing's crap; I'm crap. And as for bloody Wendy, how can she call herself a professional actress? What shall I do? I can't sleep; I look like death. Fuck! Maybe I should just swill back a bottle of temazepam and let them all go to hell.'

A voice on the line said, 'Mr Jarvis, it's Sandra in reception. You need to dial nine for an outside line.'

Now that I was on my own I was able to spend more time developing projects for television; usually through a production company with Nigel Havers, which, with remarkable originality, we called Havahall, and subsequently through my own company Whitehall Films. The agency thrived, but I was beginning to feel that familiar sensation of treading water: as the production side increased, my enthusiasm for the agency began to subside. It was difficult trying to keep both sides of the business on an even keel. Talking to an actor about his lack of work, while on a windy West Country location, filming a television drama series for ITV, was not an ideal arrangement for either the actor or myself.

'Are you in the office, Michael?'

'Of course,' I lie.

Then a noise off.

'We're going for a take now! Get ready everyone.'

'Who was that?' says the actor.

'Stephen,' I bluff.

'Why was he shouting?'

Then, 'Quiet everybody! Action!'

'What was *that*?'

'Amanda and Stephen are having a row.'

'Why are you whispering?'

'I'm not,' I whisper.

'So have you had any feedback?'

'From?'

The bell rings.

'Five-minute break everyone.'

Thank God, I can stop whispering.

'The interview.'

'Of course, yes, I think it went fine,' I reply.

'What are my chances of getting it?'

I am now struggling as I can't remember what *it* is, and the director wants to talk to me.

'Very good. I'll be with you in sec,' I say to the director.

'Fine,' says the actor. 'What, better than fifty–fifty?'

'Sorry, I was talking to someone else, but, yes, I guess about that.'

The director is looking agitated.

'So what else is happening?' asks the actor.

'Michael, I need to speak to you NOW,' says the director.

'Are you there, Michael?' asks the actor. 'Are you sure you're in the office?'

A conflict of interest, indeed, and one that I was soon to resolve.

★   ★   ★

One of my earliest outings as a producer was on a series I made for LWT called 'The Good Guys' with Nigel Havers and Keith Barron. One episode called for an attractive Sloaney girlfriend for Nigel's character, and the casting director suggested Elizabeth Hurley. I hadn't seen her work, but the part was quite small and she looked very attractive in *Spotlight*. Once we started filming, it was obvious that she wasn't a great actress, having particular difficulty with her walking. In real life the way people walk is hardly noticeable, and so it should be when acting. But some actors, the moment they are asked to walk across the room, start doing walking-acting, apparently unable to put one foot in front of another without drawing attention to their gait. Miss Hurley also tended to become very posh when delivering dialogue, which was not a problem with this particular part but did affect her audibility. Otherwise she was a joy to have around. Vivacious, attractive and full of fun – what more could Nigel, Keith and I want on a distant location in south Devon? On her last evening, having completed filming, we sat in the hotel bar drinking and Nigel suggested that we go out for dinner. Miss Hurley went upstairs for a quick change, and we thought we had struck lucky.

'Bloody attractive girl,' said Nigel. 'I think I could be in luck.'

'Actually, I think she rather fancies me,' responded Keith. 'Did you see the way she touched my knee?'

'Well, I think you're both wrong. She's had enough of actors and is looking for more of an executive type,' I said. 'She certainly gave me a very come-on kind of look as she went upstairs.'

Nigel went off to book the table, and while he was away, Miss Hurley returned.

'Look, I'm really sorry guys, but I hadn't realized that Hugh had come down from London this afternoon. He's up in my room looking for an early night.'

She gave us both a big kiss and a beaming smile, and disappeared up the stairs.

'Hugh?' I asked.

'Grant,' said Keith. 'Nice chap – her boyfriend.'

'Shit.'

'I think I'll have an early night, too,' said Keith.

So, with a couple of exceptions, Whitehall the agent became Whitehall the producer. These were good times, even if not quite fulfilling early promise; but then unfulfilled promise was perhaps a hallmark of my life.

I remember an occasion of unfulfilled promise when I visited Colin Firth on location in Amsterdam, where he was filming. I was booked into a rather seedy hotel called the Deluxe in the middle of town. Why is it that hotels called the Deluxe seldom are? Late one night, after an evening of carousing with the cast, I returned to the hotel and collected my key from the rather surly matron at the reception desk.

As I weaved my way to my lonely room, I recalled a trip to see Edward Fox in a Strindberg play at the Manchester Royal Exchange. I had been joined by an actor friend with a Don Juan reputation. When we were shown our rooms, his was clearly superior to mine, so he gallantly offered to swap.

'You're here on business; I'm just here for the ride.'

As he had insisted, I was happy to agree to the swap.

After having dinner with Edward after the performance, my friend and I stopped off at the hotel bar for a nightcap and then returned to our rooms. At two o'clock in the morning, there was a gentle tap on the door. I opened it and, through a pair of bleary eyes, saw a beautiful blonde girl standing in front of me.

'Well, hello,' I said, putting on my best Leslie Phillips drawl.

The girl explained that she had in fact come to see my actor friend.

'We changed rooms,' I replied rather dejectedly. 'He's in 296.'

She apologized for having disturbed me and disappeared down the corridor.

The following morning, my friend was sitting in the dining room, tucking into a breakfast of bacon and eggs.

'I had a caller last night,' I said. 'Did she find you OK?'

'Oh, yes, thanks. I'm sorry about that.'

'Who was she? Was she on room service?'

'No, no, she's a great girl. I met her years ago when I was filming here. She's a continuity girl. Married with a couple of kids. Usually try and see her when I'm in Manchester.'

'What, at three o'clock in the morning?'

'Her husband's a heavy sleeper.'

Unfortunately, there were no soft taps at the Deluxe – not that I was looking for Rosa Klebb from downstairs. I lay on the bed and investigated a row of buttons set into the headboard. There was one for the television, another for the radio, and one at the end provocatively labelled 'Magic Fingers', which could be activated only by the insertion of coins. I tried the television and radio first – Dutch radio was not the kind of action I was looking for – so I took the plunge and shoved a coin into the slot. The bed began to vibrate and then started to throb. The motion made me feel sick, particularly after too many brandies. I got off the bed, collapsed into a chair, and waited for the action to finish. With one minute remaining, the clock jammed and the bed continued to vibrate and throb. I walked gingerly downstairs to the reception to ask for Rosa's help. She gave me what used to be called an 'old-fashioned look'.

'I come five minutes.'

I couldn't wait.

She came into the room, kicked the bed, switched something off under the mattress and, with a heavy sigh, left the room.

I sat on the bed, and a leaflet on the bedside table caught my eye. 'AMSTERDAM, WHERE ALL YOUR FANTASIES COME TRUE'.

Not, sadly, in my case.

Richard Griffiths, Anton Rodgers, his wife Elizabeth Garvie and the theatre producer and director Jane McCulloch were sailing to New York on the *QE2* on an all-expenses-paid junket. In exchange for some very high-quality board and lodging, all they had to do was give a talk on their lives in show business. The nice lady from the *QE2*'s head office asked me if Hilary and I would like to join them and share my theatrical reminiscences with my fellow passengers. My initial response was a resounding 'no': they were the performers, not me, and I had a business to run. However, on further reflection and, with the agency taking up less of my time, I thought, why the hell not?

As the date for departure from Southampton loomed, I began to worry: I'd never done anything like this before. OK, the odd anecdote over the dinner table, but an hour's entertainment in front of an audience of strangers . . . I remembered Nigel Havers, quoting to great comic effect at my wedding, from a book called *How to be the Best Best Man*. Was there something similar devoted to witty talks on cruise liners? By the time we set sail, I had cobbled together a string of mildly amusing anecdotes and hoped that a shot of adrenalin would come to the rescue when I stood up and did my stuff.

'You're not on tomorrow, so you can just enjoy yourself,' said Brian, the entertainments manager. And enjoy ourselves we did. The food was of lavish proportions: champagne, caviar, smoked salmon, wonderful claret and burgundy. And all free.

'We really mustn't have caviar at every meal,' said Anton. We agreed, until the next meal.

We all watched Richard's show, which was a triumph. The shows were recorded and then made available, on a loop, on the in-cabin TV; so we only had to perform live once. It was an actor's dream: you could watch yourself all day and all night until you reached New York. Later that evening a note from Brian was slipped under my cabin door. 'See you at 7.45 in the theatre, and we'll have breakfast together afterwards. Brian.' Breakfast . . . They wouldn't want me to perform at 8 a.m. Surely not. I checked 'Tomorrow's Events', and there I was opening a full day of events in the theatre at 8 a.m.

I arrived the next morning at 7.45. Brian told me he would give a short opening and closing speech, and that I should talk for an hour. By eight o'clock there were two elderly ladies in the audience. By the end the numbers had swelled by a further six. At the end Brian thanked 'Mr Michael Whitelaw' for a really interesting talk (even though he had not actually stayed for it) and thanked 'everyone' for coming.

'Breakfast?' he asked. 'It went down really well, didn't it?'

As I stepped down from the stage into the auditorium, an elderly man — small, grey-haired and American — approached me.

'Wonderful, sir,' he muttered. 'Can we talk about a book?'

'That's more like it,' I thought. 'A book, now that's what I should be doing — *writing* about my life in show business — not stringing together anecdotes for a bunch of insomniacs on the *QE2* in return for some free caviar.'

'I have a breakfast meeting,' I said rather grandly.

'Could we meet later?' he said.

'Certainly,' I replied.

'Let's say eleven o'clock in the Coffee House. Oh, and my name is Joe Rubens.'

After an overly long breakfast, Brian told me his deeply uninteresting life story, and that he was leaving his job at the end of the summer to try his luck as an actor.

'Could I come and see you?' he asked.

I explained that I had more clients than I could cope with, and anyway I was planning to retire soon.

'I just need someone to get me on the first rung of the ladder.'

Brian was not a man in the prime of his life, despite having honey-blond hair and an impressive suntan, and must have been well into his fifties — rather late in the day to be hitting the first rung of the ladder. I told him

'By eight o'clock there were two elderly ladies in the audience'

to ring me when he had left the ship, and I would suggest a few agents to him. I then went to the Coffee House to meet Mr Rubens and talk about myself for a change. Book signings, serializations, talk-show interviews, this could be the beginning of another phase of my life: maybe the big one that I'd been waiting for.

Joe was sitting at a corner table.

'Mike, what'll it be?' he asked.

'Coffee please, Joe. Cappuccino, if they've got it.'

I sat down opposite him. On the table was a roughly wrapped brown package.

'So can we talk?' he asked.

'Certainly, Joe, that's why I am here. Let's talk books.'

'The thing is, Mike, I've written a book, which, I think if handled properly, could be very big and I'd love you to read it, and give me your take on it.'

He had written a book; I couldn't believe it.

He then opened the parcel and handed me a yellowing bunch of three or four hundred pages, tied together with an elastic band.

'*The Bermuda Triangle Murders*,' he said. 'My latest story in the Jack Delaney Mystery series.' He told me he had written them over the previous twenty years and had decided the time was right to be published. 'They are kind of Raymond Chandler meets Agatha Christie, with a hint of Daphne du Maurier,' he said modestly. 'When I heard you talking about your clients so fondly, I thought this is the man to handle my writing.'

I explained that I was not a literary agent.

'Not a problem,' he replied. 'I've had various literary agents in the States and they've all been shit, which is basically why I've never had any of my work published. I think you are the man to do it for me.'

I tried to steer the conversation off this ludicrous book in its nasty crumpled brown paper. 'Do you travel on the *QE2* often?' I asked.

'Yes, I do. I actually work on the ship.'

'Oh, in what capacity?'

'I'm a host: that is to say I entertain the middle-aged and elderly ladies who regularly sail with us.'

'Doing what?'

'As a dance partner, bridge player, on the gaming tables, as a dinner guest, that kind of thing.'

'And they pay you for this?'

'Well I get tips from them, but I am paid by the ship's owners . . . nothing very substantial. I consider being a host my hobby and writing my profession.'

I suspected the reality was probably the other way round. Luckily, Hilary appeared to remind me that we had agreed to meet Richard for a drink before lunch.

'Will you try and read the book before we get to New York? Maybe we could then meet up and discuss where we go from there.'

I knew exactly where I was going: to avoid Joe Rubens at all costs for the rest of the trip. I read *The Bermuda Triangle Murders* in my cabin that evening, at least the first chapter anyway. It was like a child's essay, full of spelling mistakes, and with absolutely no literary merit. I left it in my cabin in New York in the hope that someone would pick it up and return it to Mr Rubens.

Back in London I received a string of letters from him demanding the return of his manuscript. He was concerned that I was trying to film it behind his back. Some chance. He then told me that the manuscript was in fact the only copy of his book and, unless I returned it forthwith, he would put his lawyers on to me. I told him that to have given the only copy of his life's work to a complete stranger on the high seas was perhaps a trifle foolish, and directed him and his lawyers to the lost property office of the *QE2*. Thankfully, I never heard from him again.

I also discovered on my return that one of my clients had left me, though, sadly, not for another agent. The Putney Vale Crematorium has two chapels with a communal porch. I was standing in the porch talking to an actor whom I vaguely knew, when we were called into the service. I hadn't been the actor's agent whose funeral it was for long and had in fact met him only once, so I was surprised when his wife had called me a week or two earlier and asked me if I would say a few words about him. It was difficult to refuse but not an easy call. 'I met Richard once and he seemed like a nice chap,' and so on. I was looking around the sparsely filled chapel for

Richard's wife but as I'd never met her, it was a difficult task, and then the piped music started playing 'The Lord is My Shepherd' and the undertakers walked in with the coffin. After the prayers and another hymn, the vicar rose to his feet and starting addressing us in suitably funereal tones: 'Mary was a much loved and respected doctor whose life was cut tragically short by . . .'

Mary? Who the hell was Mary?! What was Mary doing in Richard's coffin? I looked around at the small congregation – certainly no recognizable faces. I whispered to my actor friend, 'This is Richard's funeral, isn't it?'

'No,' he replied, 'Mary Wadey, my doctor; I think he's in the other chapel.'

I couldn't leave until the end of the vicar's address, which went on for ever, but finally crept out, followed by a chorus of tuts and accusatory looks.

I ran across the porch and gently opened the door of the adjoining chapel, which made the sort of noise one associates with the front door of Count Dracula's castle in Transylvania. The service was by now almost halfway through, the chapel was packed and more accusatory stares greeted my arrival. A woman grabbed me just as I was about to sit down and led me to the only empty seat in the front row marked 'Reserved for Speaker'. The woman turned out to be Richard's wife, and was clearly cross, flustered and emotional.

'We thought you weren't going to show up. You're on next. My niece was standing by to take your place but she has a terrible cold and has almost lost her voice. Thank God you've got here.'

There wasn't time to explain why I hadn't shown up earlier, as I was then on my feet behind the lectern telling the congregation what a fine actor Richard was and what a fine man he was too. A rare combination. I then reminisced about various productions he'd been in, which I'd never seen but which I'd taken off his CV, and ended with a glowing tribute to his wife (whose name I completely forgot), who had helped him through his last brave battle with the illness that had dogged him for the last year. That, of course, was why I didn't really know him and he never actually worked or even went up for a job during our short time together. After the service, I didn't linger in the porch as the other funeral had come out and I didn't think I could cope with two sets of death stares.

A reception was being held at a hotel nearby and I was the second person to arrive. An elderly man, rather scruffily dressed for the occasion I thought, was standing in the middle of the room munching on a sausage roll. I thought it would be rude not to speak to him; he was at least giving me friendly looks, which had been in short supply over the past few hours.

'I didn't actually get to the crematorium. I came straight here.'

'Did you know Richard well?' I asked.

'Oh no, I never met him but I admired his work enormously. I read about the service in the paper and as we're both from Peterborough I thought I'd come and pay my respects. But I got held up on the A1 so I came straight to the reception. These sausage rolls are nice. You were an old friend, presumably?'

'No, not really, but he was a fine actor.'

'Indeed he was. Wasn't he in that series "Duty Free", played the posh chap married to the blonde?'

'No, I don't think so. Wasn't that Neil Stacy?'

'I'm sure it was Richard,' he said. 'And didn't Penelope Keith play the blonde?'

As he headed off towards a tray of vol-au-vents, the room began to fill up. I sneaked off as Richard's admirer was offering them to the family.

At the best of times, Croydon isn't a great proposition. In the *Domesday Book* it is referred to as Croindene, the valley where wild saffron grows. Nine hundred years later, the scent in the car park of the Fairfields Hall was less fragrant, more fungal. But at least the car park was full, which was encouraging as the client I had come to see was on a percentage of the box office.

Once inside the theatre I realized that the Fairfields had two separate auditoriums: one for live music, the other, the Ashcroft, for straight plays. The Manfreds and the Bay City Rollers were sold out; not so Leslie Grantham, in Stephen King's aptly named thriller *Misery*. As Grantham's character was in the process of having his foot cut off, the modest audience was about to lose two of its members.

'I can't take any more of this,' said the woman to her husband, as they stomped up the gangway towards the exit sign.

'That's why we're fucking leaving,' he replied.

They had been sitting in the front row of the stalls, so this exchange was clearly audible to everyone: more audible, in fact, than anything coming from the stage.

'And anyway you told me it was Leslie Crowther.'

'Don't be daft,' she shouted, 'he's dead.'

'I wish I was,' said the man sitting in front of me.

After the play, we ended up in the only open eating house in town, a grim Italian pizzeria, and discussed the play in more detail than it deserved. My new assistant, who in the short time she had worked for me appeared to have only one topic of conversation, namely when she was going to get a pay rise, launched herself into a detailed analysis of Leslie's American accent. I hadn't actually realized that he was playing American and now understood why the play was so difficult to understand. Leslie was a master of many things, but accents were not among them.

My visit to Croydon gave me the final nudge I needed. After a relaxing and contemplative family holiday on the beautiful island of Jamaica, I made up my mind that it was time for me to take down my shingle and move on. I was fortunate to have prospered in the shark-infested waters of the agency business for over thirty-five years and, if I never quite achieved my mother's aspirations, I certainly had an enormous amount of fun trying.

10

Poacher Turned Gamekeeper

As I became more and more involved in the production side of the business, it began to dawn on me how aggravating most actors' agents were. 'A person who lives off others' is the *Oxford Dictionary* definition of a parasite: it might equally apply to an agent, well from a producer's standpoint anyway. So you've spent many creative months with writers, co-producers and directors bringing your project to fruition, and the time has arrived for you to start talking to actors' agents. And all they want to talk about is money.

Nothing creative, nothing constructive to say, just ludicrous financial demands for their clients who, when you meet them without their agents, have offered to do the job for nothing, such is their boundless enthusiasm for it. But the moment the bloody agent gets his nose into it all, forget about the wonderful part, the amazing script, the sensitive director (not to mention the brilliant producer); it's just all about the money.

'You should be paying me for offering your client a fucking good job,' I want to say. 'Let's face it, nobody else is.' But I don't because I'm the producer, and I want to keep in with the agent and have him on my side in case there's trouble further down the line.

'And what about expenses?' asks the agent. Expenses, and he hasn't even mentioned the script yet. 'And what kind of profit participation were you thinking of?'

He doesn't seriously think I'm going to give his client a percentage of the profits. He'll be asking for cast approval next.

'And we'll want cast approval of course. Well, for the principal roles anyway . . .'

That's generous.

'And, of course, the part needs work done on it . . .'

This usually means that his client wants his part made bigger and, as a result, the other parts made smaller. Probably not the time to go into any detail on this as the agent won't have read the script anyway. So I don't say, 'What bits?'

And then.

'And what about billing? He'd obviously want first solo star . . .'

Note the 'obviously' dropped in here.

'And nobody else billed in the same-size type, colour or prominence. Single line above the title.'

Perhaps he should hold out for a one-man show, I think.

One of my earliest duties as an agent at ICM was to walk up Shaftesbury Avenue, armed with a Stanley Powerlock Ruler, and measure the size of lettering for one of Olive Harding's clients outside the Queens Theatre. Olive was a fearsome agent with a Rottweiler approach to representation; and if I reported back as much as a quarter-inch discrepancy in the client's contractual billing size, the entire front of house would have to be dismantled and reassembled within forty-eight hours, otherwise she would withdraw her client's services.

Eventually and despite his totally destructive contribution to the project, an agreed contract is sent to the agent for the actor's signature.

'There are some loose ends to tie up,' he says.

'Like?'

'Personal dresser, voice coach, make-up artist, driver, masseur – you know, just the bits and pieces. And, of course, a pair of first-class round trips for the actor's wife, and a pair for his agent . . .' Of course.

Agents are nothing but trouble. Actors are a complete joy compared with their agents.

Believe me . . . I know.